Barndominium Floor Plans and Designs

Extensive Barndominium Plans and Designs Selections with Garage for Your Next Barn Home Ideas

Mary Decor

Copyright © Mary Décor 2022

All rights reserved. This book is copyright and no part of it may be reproduced, distributed, or transmitted in any form or by any means, including photocopying, recording, or other electronic or mechanical methods, without the prior written permission of the publisher, except in the case of brief quotations embodied in critical reviews and certain other non commercial uses permitted by copyright law.

Printed in the United States of America

Copyright © 2022

Contents

Plan for a Rustic Ranch House with Cathedral Ceilings and a Wide Front Porch	3
Floor Plan	7
Plan details	8
4-Bedroom Modern Farmhouse Barndominium with Large Bonus Room over Garage	10
Deluxe Barndominium with 2-Story Living Room	16
Barndominium-style House Plan with Soaring Cathedral Ceiling with Exposed Beams	22
Barndominium-style House Plan with Home Office and Two-story Great Room	27
Barndominium with Wraparound Porch and 2-Story Living Room	33
Lakefront Home with a Massive Enclosed Deck	42
One-story Country Lake House Design with an Enormous Encircling Deck	50
Floor Plan	55
Plan details	57
New American Garage Apartment Plan with Barndominium Styling	59
Three-Bedroom One-Story Modern Farmhouse	64
Floor Plan	68
Plan details	70
Barn-Style Garage with Apartment Above	72
Floor Plan	76
Plan details	78
Modern Mountain House Plan with Great Room Open to Upstairs Loft	80
Rustic Barndominium with Loft Overlooking Great Room Below	88
Main Level	89
Charming Farmhouse Barndominium with Two Bedrooms	93
Floor Plan	95

Plan details	97
Rustic Ranch Home Plan with Cathedral Ceilings and a Broad Front Porch	99
Rustic Shop House with Vaulted Great Room and Covered Outdoor Spaces	103
Barn-Style Garage with Apartment Above	107
Barndominium with a Front Wrapping Porch	111
Charming Farmhouse Barndominium with Two Bedrooms	116
Floor Plan	118
Plan details	120
Expanded Barn-Style Garage with Tractor Port	122
Main Level	123
2nd Floor	124
The Garage Resembles A Barn With A Vaulted Workshop, Dog Run, Side Porch, And Bonus Space	127
Floor Plan	130
Plan details	132
Exclusive 5-Bedroom Modern Farmhouse Plan with Upstairs Master Suite and Laundry	134
Floor Plan	135
2nd Floor	136
4-Bed Country Craftsman Plan with Open Concept Living Space	139
Floor Plan	140
2nd Floor	141

Plan for a Rustic Ranch House with Cathedral Ceilings and a Wide Front Porch

We provide a wide variety of barn homes, featuring carriage houses and year-round dwellings. Use our collection as a reference point for your new home, whether you're building in the country, a picturesque New England town, or truly prefer the style of a barn.

• The exterior of this exquisite 3-bedroom, 1-story barndominium house plan is composed of stone, a metal roof, wood beams, and board-and-batten siding.

• A spacious covered entrance porch with a cathedral ceiling leads to an open floor layout inside.

• The dining area, kitchen, and family room are all situated beneath a soaring cathedral ceiling, which creates the impression of a spacious interior. The fireplace in the family room is flanked by built-in bookcases, and the kitchen island has a snack bar. The fireplace in the family room is flanked by built-in bookcases, and the kitchen island has a snack bar.

• The master bedroom is tucked away on the left side of the house for privacy and includes a gorgeous tray ceiling. The master bathroom has separate vanities, a private toilet area, a linen closet, and a large walk-in closet. Two bedrooms share a hall bathroom with dual vanities that is centrally located in the property.

1,695	3	2	1
Heated S.F.	Beds	Baths	Stories

Floor Plan

Main Level

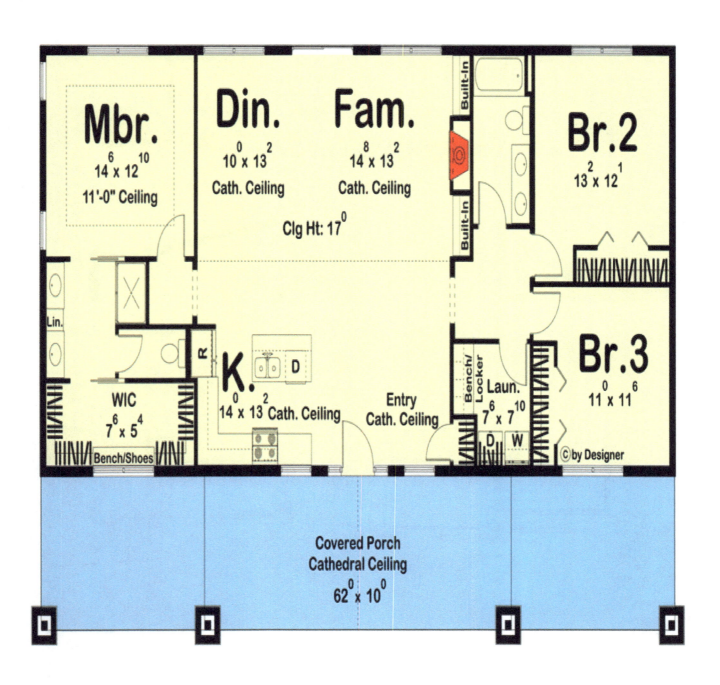

Plan details

Square Footage Breakdown

Total Heated Area:	1,695 sq. ft.
1st Floor:	1,695 sq. ft.
Porch, Front:	618 sq. ft.

Dimensions

Width:	62' 0"
Depth:	38' 0"
Max Ridge Height:	21' 0"

Beds/Baths

Bedrooms:	3
Full Bathrooms:	2

Ceiling Heights

Floor / Height:	First Floor / 10' 0"

Foundation Type

Standard Foundations:	Slab
Optional Foundations:	Basement, Crawl, Walkout

Roof Details

Primary Pitch: 8 on 12

Secondary Pitch: 3 on 12

Framing Type: Stick

Exterior Walls

Standard Type(s): 2x6

4-Bedroom Modern Farmhouse Barndominium with Large Bonus Room over Garage

With board-and-batten siding, a metal roof, wooden beams, and wooden garage doors, the outside of this Barndominium represents a Modern Farmhouse style.

A large, wraparound covered front porch creates an inviting ambiance for guests. Upon entering the house, you will see a spacious, open plan. The spacious room features a fireplace flanked by French doors that lead to the covered porch and is placed beneath a two-story cathedral ceiling.

The kitchen has a large island with a snack bar and a large walk-in pantry. For optimal solitude, and privacy, the master suite is positioned in the property's rear on the main level. The ceiling of the master bedroom is ornamented with troughs. The master bathroom features separate vanities, a soaking tub, and a large walk-in closet with laundry room access.

You will see three additional bedrooms above. In a jack-and-jill design, the second and third bedrooms have the same bathroom. The fourth bedroom and loft share a hall bathroom located in the center of the hallway. A huge loft overlooks the primary living area. Back on the main level, the three-car garage offers a drive-through bay. A convenient mudroom with a catch-all and coat closet gives access from the residence to the garage.

Floor Plan

Main Level

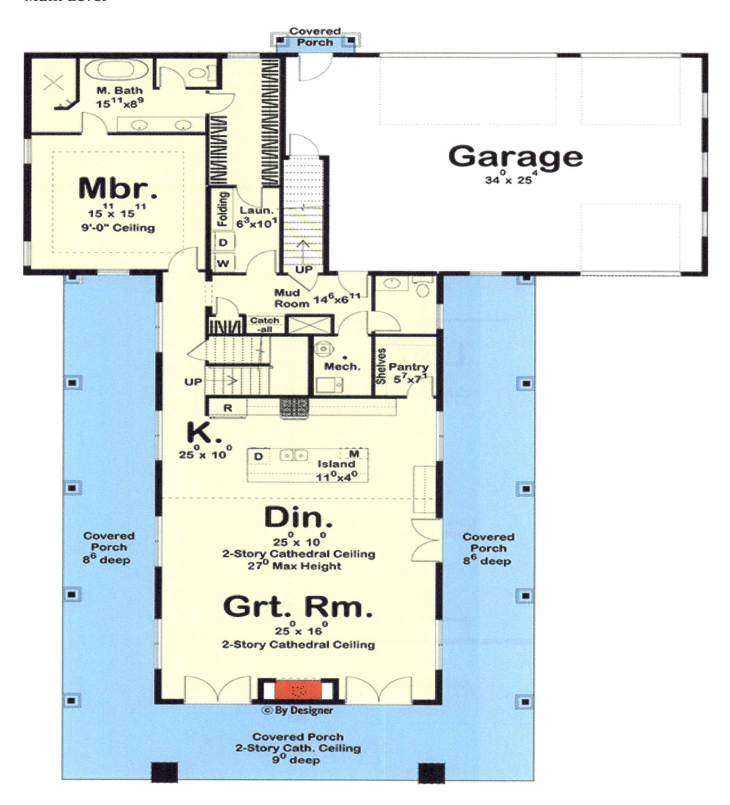

Second Floor

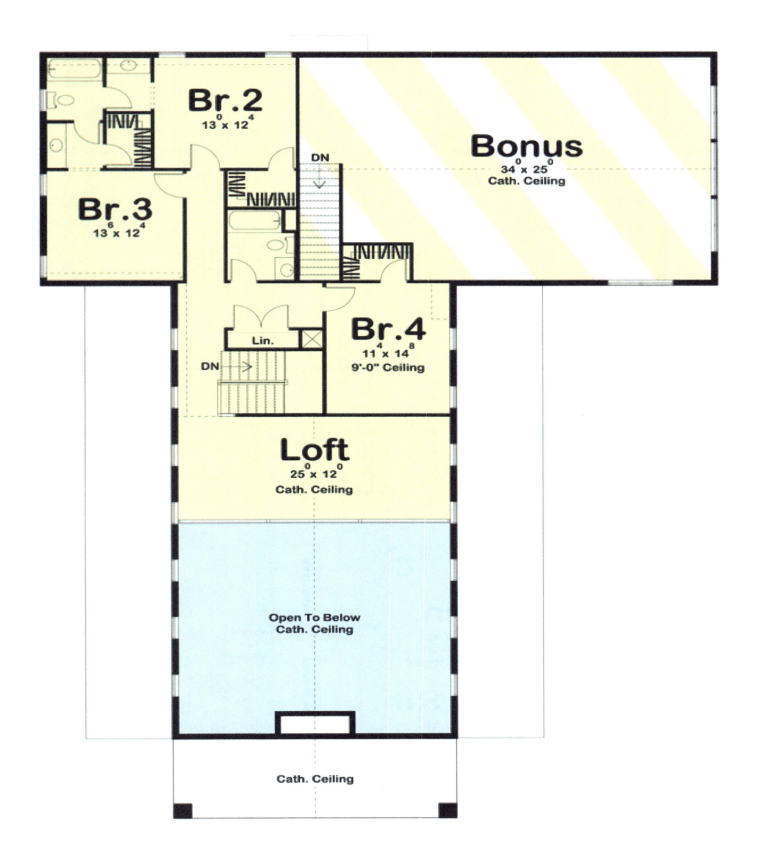

Plan Details

Square Footage Breakdown

Total Heated Area:	3,205 sq. ft.
1st Floor:	1,943 sq. ft.
2nd Floor:	1,262 sq. ft.
Porch, Combined:	1,058 sq. ft.
Bonus:	850 sq. ft.

Dimensions

Width	62' 0"
Depth	86' 0"
Max Ridge Height	32' 0"

Beds/Baths

Bedrooms	4
Full Bathrooms	3
Half Bathrooms	1

Foundation type

Standard Foundations	Slab
Optional Foundations	Walkout, Crawl, Basement

Garage

Type	Attached
Area	937 sq. ft.
Count	3 cars
Entry Location	Rear, Front

Exterior walls

Standard Type(s)	2x6

Ceiling Heights

Floor / Height	First Floor / 9' 0"
	Second Floor / 8' 0"

Roof Details

Primary Pitch	12 On 12
Secondary Pitch	4 On 12
Framing Type	Truss

Deluxe Barndominium with 2-Story Living Room

This premium Barndominium type structure plan (stick-framing) incorporates board-and-batten siding that replicates the ribbed metal roof, an architectural trend sweeping rural America.

On the right side of this plan is a 1,480-square-foot garage with a powder room, an overhead door on the front elevation, and a barn door on the back. The living space is surrounded by a porch, which leads to the kitchen; this is an ideal floor plan for entertaining. The master bedroom on the main floor features a tiled shower in the adjoining bathroom and a direct route to the laundry room. There is a huge loft and two bedrooms that share a full bathroom on the second floor.

Floor Plan

Main Level

Second Floor

Basement Option

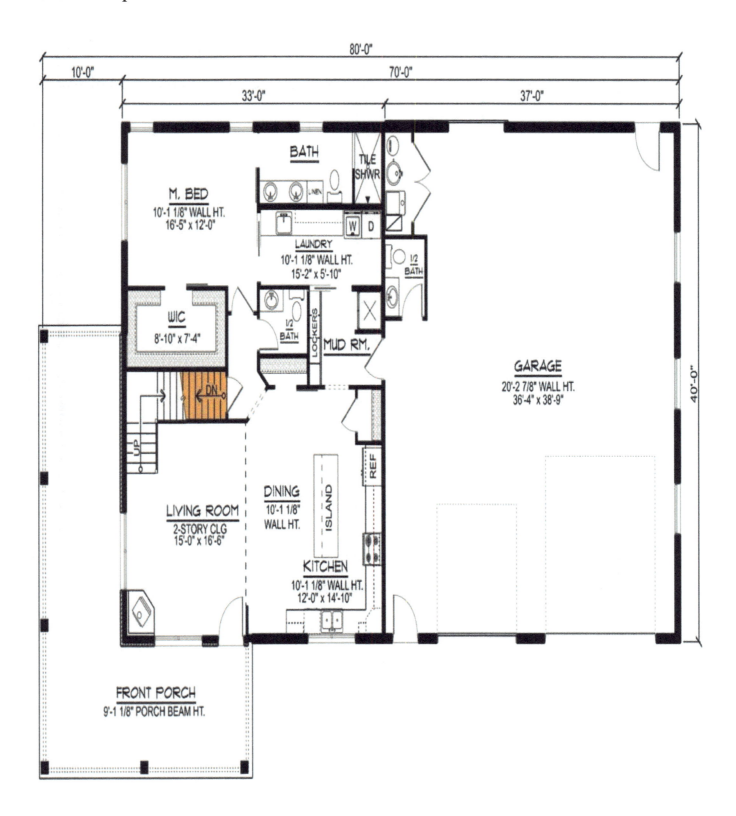

Square Footage Breakdown

Total Heated Area:	2,311 sq. ft.
1st Floor:	1,320 sq. ft.
2nd Floor:	991 sq. ft.
Porch, Combined:	500 sq. ft.

Dimensions

Width	80' 0"
Depth	50' 0"
Max Ridge Height	27' 5"

Beds/Baths

Bedrooms	3
Full Bathrooms	2
Half Bathrooms	1

Foundation type

Standard Foundations	Slab
Optional Foundations	Walkout, Crawl, Basement

Garage

Type	Attached
Area	1480 sq. ft.
Count	2 cars
Entry	Front

Exterior walls

Standard Type(s)	2x6

Ceiling Heights

Framing Type:Truss

Floor / Height	First Floor / 10' 0"
	Second Floor / 9' 0"

Roof Details

Primary Pitch	4 On 12
Framing Type	Truss

Barndominium-style House Plan with Soaring Cathedral Ceiling with Exposed Beams

This barndominium-style (built using traditional construction) 3-bedroom floor plan offers an attractive board and batten exterior, a standing seam metal roof, and a wide pergola. Dual-paned windows aid in bringing the outdoors within.

The principal interior living space features an open layout. The 12-foot-tall walls give the impression that the entire residence is huge. Under a vaulted cathedral ceiling with exposed beams are the living room, dining area, and kitchen. The living room is heated by a fireplace flanked by bookcases that are built-in. A home office is adjacent to the living space and features a built-in desk.

The kitchen features a large island with a snack bar. In addition, the kitchen has a substantial walk-in pantry with built-in shelving. A large sliding glass door connects the dining area to the terrace's roof.

Its master suite is located on the left side of the house and features a beautiful tray ceiling. The master bathroom is equipped with a soaking tub, vanities, a doored toilet area, and a walk-in shower. A coffee bar in the master suite provides direct access to a private covered patio in the backyard.

Each of the second and third bedrooms has its own walk-in closet and shares a Jack-and-Jill bathroom. The colossal three-car garage offers a massive RV area with a large door. The garage is accessible by a convenient mudroom with a seat and lockers.

Floor Plans

Main Level

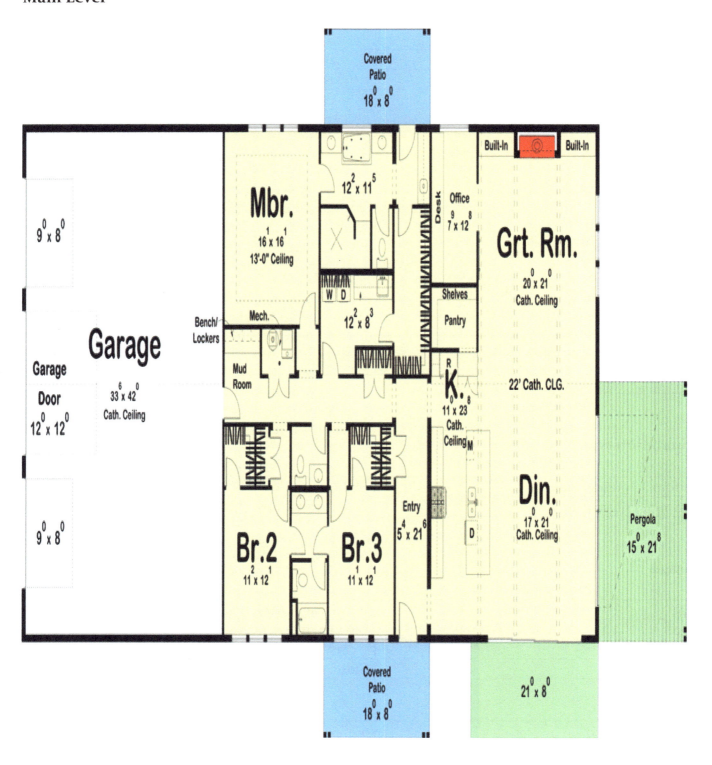

Plan Details

Square Footage Breakage

Total Heated Area:	2,752 sq. ft.
1st Floor:	2,752 sq. ft.
Porch, Rear	144 sq. ft.
Porch, Front	144 sq. ft.

Dimensions

Width	113' 0"
Depth	59' 0"
Max Ridge Height	24' 0"

Beds/Baths

Bedrooms	3
Full Bathrooms	2
Half Bathrooms	1

Foundation type

Standard Foundations	Slab
Optional Foundations	Basement, Crawl, Walkout

Garage

Type	RV Garage, Attached
Area	1462 sq. ft.
Count	3 cars
Entry Location	Side

Exterior walls

Standard Type(s)	2x6

Ceiling Heights

| Floor / Height | First Floor / 12' 0" |

Roof Details

Primary Pitch	6 On 12
Secondary Pitch	0 On 12
Framing Type	Truss

Barndominium-style House Plan with Home Office and Two-story Great Room

This remarkable barndominium-style house plan features a barn-like facade with board-and-batten siding, big windows, and barn doors. Just inside the home's side entrance is a functional office that is ideal for those who work from home.

In a large, open concept, the living room, dining area and kitchen flow together smoothly. The great room's lofty ceilings make a room feel expansive. The living room's fireplace is surrounded by built-in bookcases. There is a huge island as well as a walk-in pantry in the kitchen.

For solitude, the master suite is located to the right of the house. The master bathroom features a soaking tub, dual vanities, a walk-in shower and a private commode. The master bedroom closet provides easy passageway to the laundry room.

Here on the left side of the residence, bedrooms two and three share a hall bathroom with the primary living area. A spectacular loft overlooks the living room. The home's enormous three-car garage has a cathedral ceiling and is accessible via a mud room with a bench and lockers.

Floor Plan

Main Level

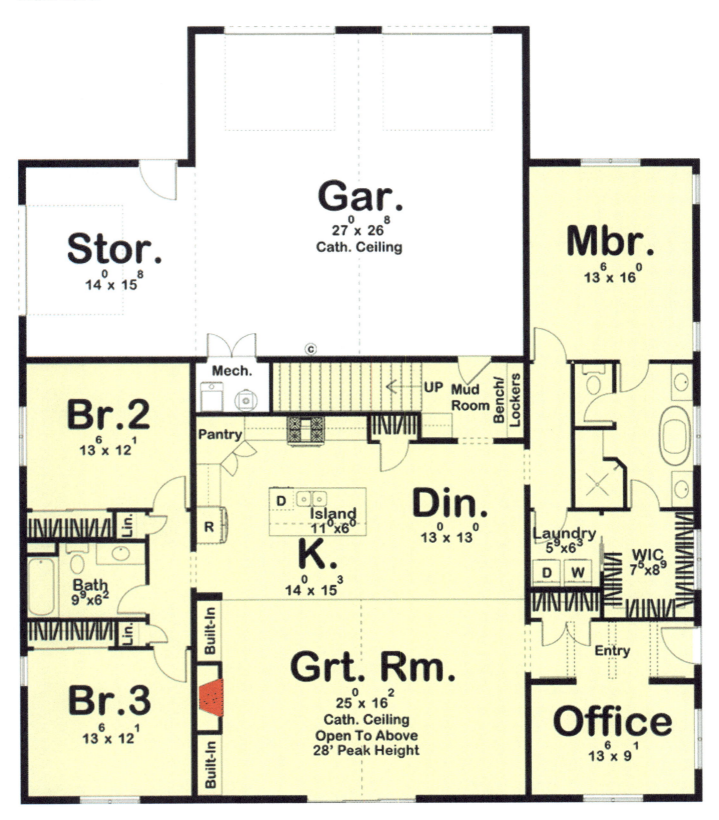

Second Floor

Main Level- Basement Stair Location

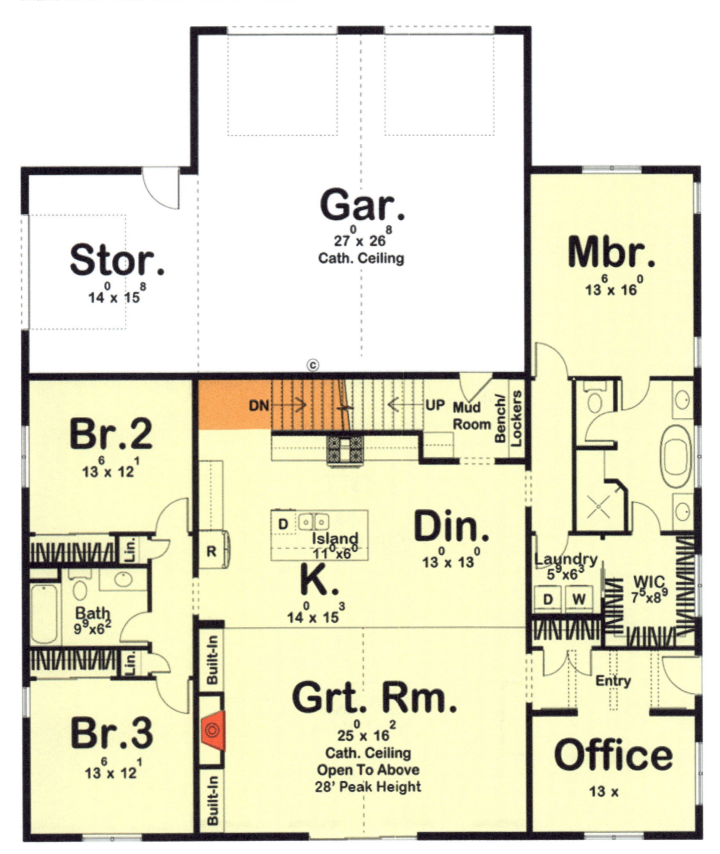

31

Plan Details

Square Footage Breakage

Total Heated Area:	2,810 sq. ft.
1st Floor:	2,297 sq. ft.
2nd Floor	513 sq. ft.

Dimensions

Width	56' 0"
Depth	64' 0"
Max Ridge Height	31' 0"

Beds/Baths

Bedrooms	3
Full Bathrooms	2

Foundation type

Standard Foundations	Slab
Optional Foundations	Basement, Crawl, Walkout

Garage

Type	Attached
Area	979 sq. ft.
Count	3 cars
Entry Location	Rear

Exterior walls

Standard Type(s)	2x6

Roof Details

Primary Pitch	10 On 12
Secondary Pitch	3 On 12
Framing Type	Truss

Barndominium with Wraparound Porch and 2-Story Living Room

- Board-and-batten siding matches the corrugated metal roof on the exterior of this opulent Barndominium-style house plan (stick-framing); an architectural trend sweeping rural America.

- The 1,480-square-foot garage, complete with a powder room, a wide overhead door on the front elevation, and a barn door on the back, is positioned on the right side of this design.

A porch wraps around the living area, which is connected to the kitchen; a terrific layout for entertaining.

- The master bedroom is located on the main floor and includes a tiled shower and direct access to the laundry area in the adjacent bathroom. • The second story offers a large loft and two bedrooms that share a large bathroom.

Floor Plan

Main Level

2nd Floor

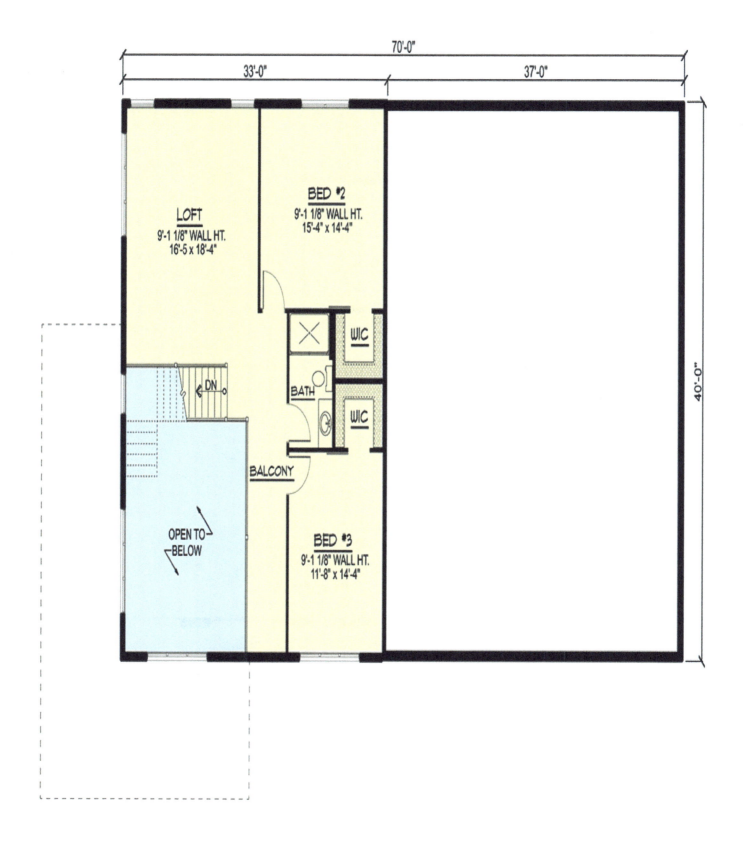

Basement Option

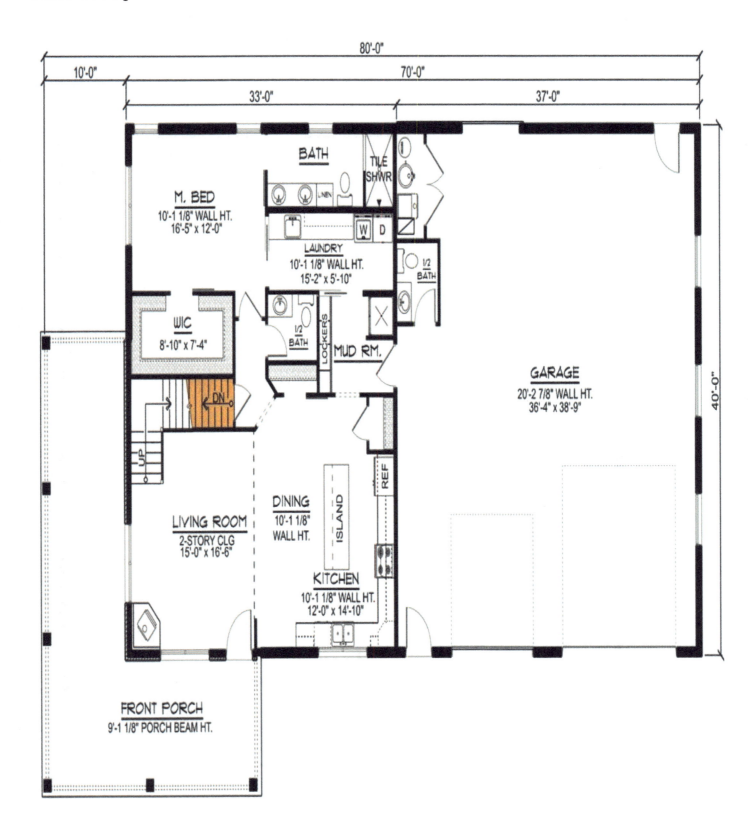

Plan details

Square Footage Breakdown

Total Heated Area:	2,311 sq. ft.
1st Floor:	1,320 sq. ft.
2nd Floor:	991 sq. ft.
Porch, Front:	500 sq. ft.

Dimensions

Width:	80' 0"
Depth:	50' 0"
Max Ridge Height:	27' 5"

Beds/Baths

Bedrooms:	3
Full Bathrooms:	2
Half Bathrooms:	1

Garage

Type:	Attached
Area:	1480 sq. ft.
Count:	2 cars
Entry Location:	Front

Foundation Type

Standard Foundations: Slab

Optional Foundations: Walkout, Crawl, Basement

Ceiling Heights

Floor / Height:

First Floor / 10' 0"
Second Floor / 9' 0"

Exterior Walls

Standard Type(s): 2x6

Roof Details

Primary Pitch: 4 on 12

Framing Type: Truss

Lakefront Home with a Massive Enclosed Deck

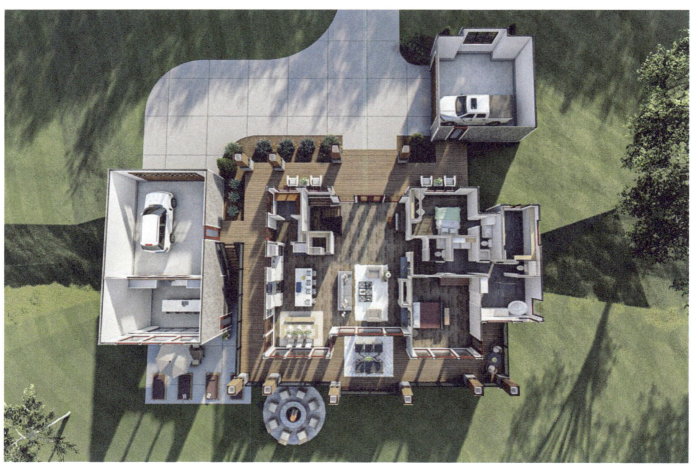

2,150	2-5	2.5 - 4.5	1	4
Heated S.F.	Beds	Baths	Stories	Cars

• This lake house design features a generous amount of outdoor living area. The appeal of the outside is contributed to by a combination of shake siding, wooden beams, and large windows. This residence is easily distinguished from others by its split garage. • Upon entering the home, you will see a large foyer with a cathedral ceiling that stretches into the great room.

•The living area features a fireplace with built-in bookcases. Kitchen and dining space are accessible from the living room. A huge walk-in pantry and a substantial island with a snack bar are featured in the kitchen. Behind the kitchen, there is a charming office with a desk.

• On the residence's left side are two bedrooms. The master bedroom has a large bathroom with two vanities, a wet area, a private toilet, and a large walk-in closet. Additionally, the second bedroom has its own bathroom.

•A finished basement adds 2,072 square feet of finished space and amenities such as a movie room with an elevated seating platform, a leisure area, 3 additional bedrooms, an additional family room, and a mudroom with a bathroom that enables you to shower as you enter from the garage's water; a lakeside bar provides access to the water for outdoor entertainment.

Floor Plan

Main Level

Optional Lower Level Layout (plus $250)

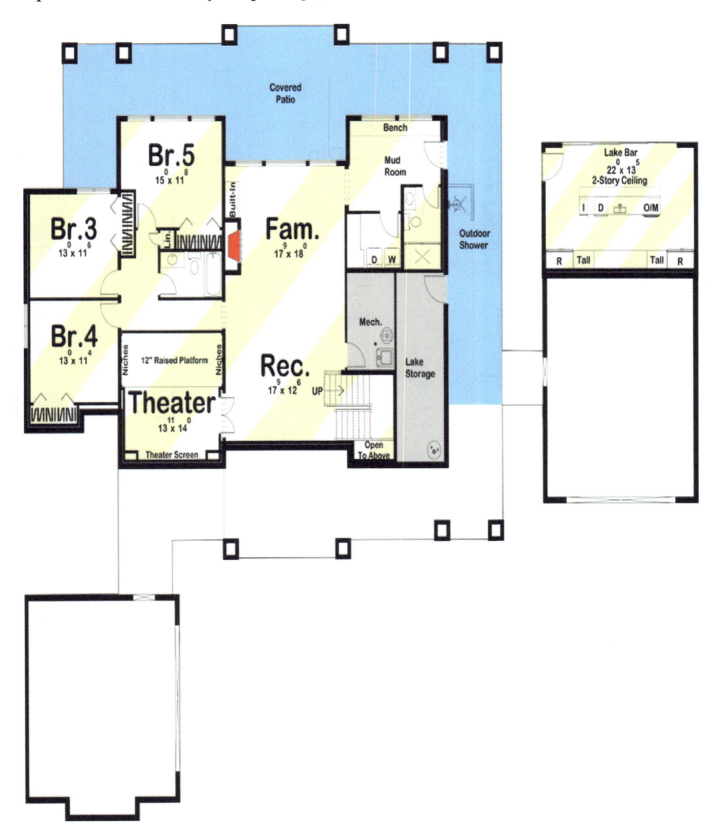

Plan details

Square Footage Breakdown

Total Heated Area:	2,150 sq. ft.
1st Floor:	2,150 sq. ft.
Optional Lower Level:	2,072 sq. ft.

Dimensions

Width:	100' 0"
Depth:	88' 0"
Max Ridge Height:	26' 0"

Beds/Baths

Bedrooms:	2, 3, 4, or 5
Full Bathrooms:	2, 3, or 4
Half Bathrooms:	1

Garage

Type:	Detached
Area:	1126 sq. ft.
Count:	4 cars
Entry Location:	Courtyard, Front

Foundation Type

Standard Foundations: Walkout

Optional Foundations: Slab, Crawl, Basement

Ceiling Heights

Floor / Height:

Lower Level / 9' 0"
First Floor / 10' 0"

Exterior Walls

Standard Type(s): 2x4

Optional Type(s): 2x6

Roof Details

Primary Pitch: 8 on 12

Secondary Pitch: 10 on 12

One-story Country Lake House Design with an Enormous Encircling Deck

1,802	2-3	2.5 - 3.5	1	2
Heated S.F.	Beds	Baths	Stories	Cars

- This aesthetically pleasing, one-story, country lake house design incorporates textured shakes beneath gabled roof lines. The huge, covered, wraparound deck takes up more than half of the outside of the house and has multiple entrances. The covered deck and covered porch give you a total of 1,802 square feet of outdoor space.

- Upon entering, the open floor plan features a fireplace with surrounding built-ins on one end and a chef's kitchen on the other. The cathedral ceiling enhances the elegance of the living area.

- Behind the kitchen is the master bedroom, which opens onto a 194-square-foot, insect-free, screened deck for outdoor enjoyment. The en suite bathroom features five fixtures and a spacious walk-in closet.

- A second bedroom with access to a full bathroom is available across the hall.

- The double garage is attached to the home's front and enters into a mudroom/laundry area with a coat closet.

Floor Plan

Main Level

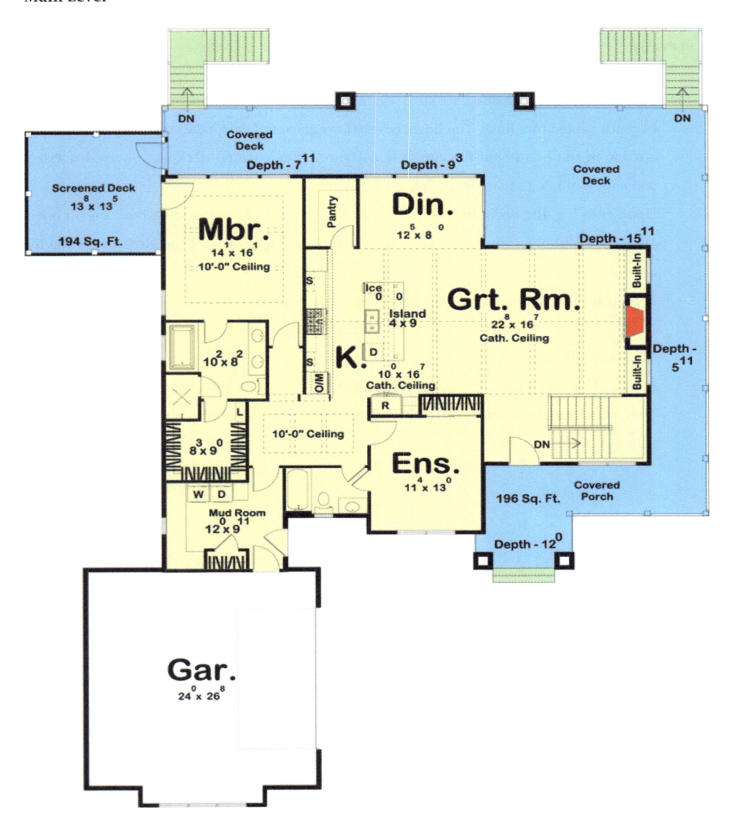

Optional Lower Level Layout (Adding $250)

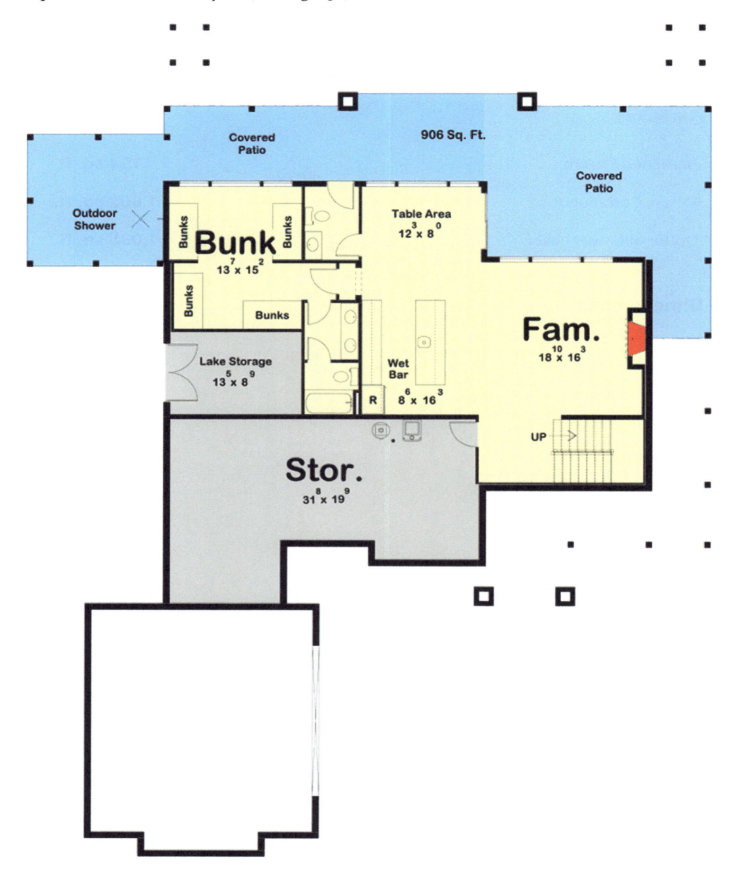

Plan details

Square Footage Breakdown

Total Heated Area:	1,802 sq. ft.
1st Floor:	1,802 sq. ft.
Screened Porch:	194 sq. ft.
Porch, Combined:	1,802 sq. ft.
Optional Lower Level:	1,035 sq. ft.

Dimensions

Width:	70' 0"
Depth:	89' 0"

Beds/Baths

Bedrooms:	2 or 3
Full Bathrooms:	2 or 3
Half Bathrooms:	1

Garage

Type:	Attached
Area:	617 sq. ft.
Count:	2 cars
Entry Location:	Courtyard

Foundation Type

Standard Foundations:	Walkout
Optional Foundations:	Slab, Basement, Crawl

Ceiling Heights

Floor / Height:	Lower Level / 9' 0" First Floor / 9' 0"

Exterior Walls

Standard Type(s):	2x4
Optional Type(s):	2x6

Roof Details

Primary Pitch:	6 on 12
Secondary Pitch:	10 on 12

New American Garage Apartment Plan with Barndominium Styling

This 2-story carriage home layout fuses New American design with Barndominium. The exterior features attractive wood accents and board-and-batten garage doors.

This garage apartment has a three-car garage just on the main level and an apartment on the upper level. The living area and kitchen are open to one another. There is an island as well as a walk-in pantry in the kitchen.

Floor Plans

Main Levels

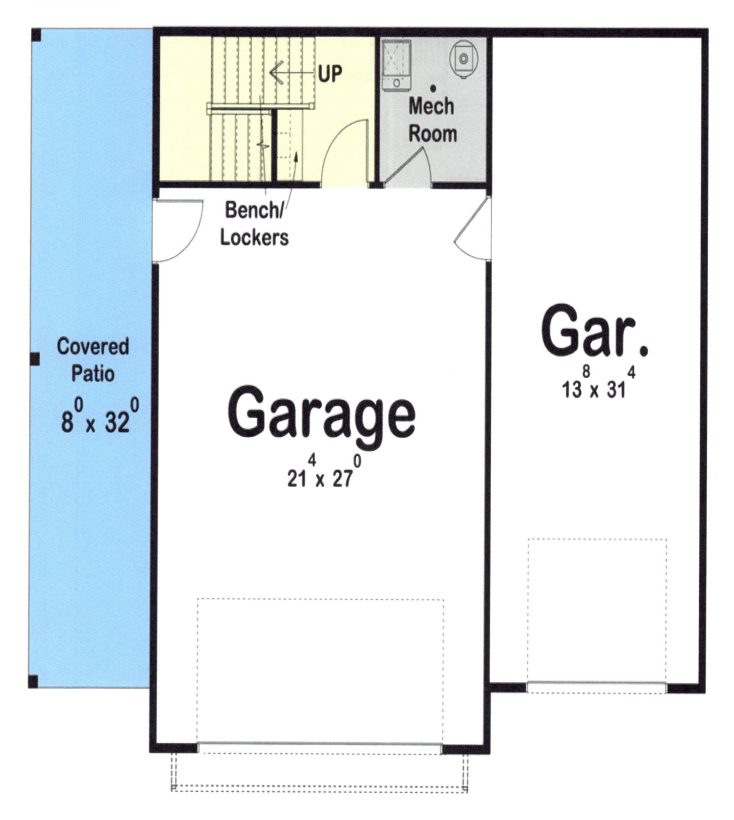

Second Floor

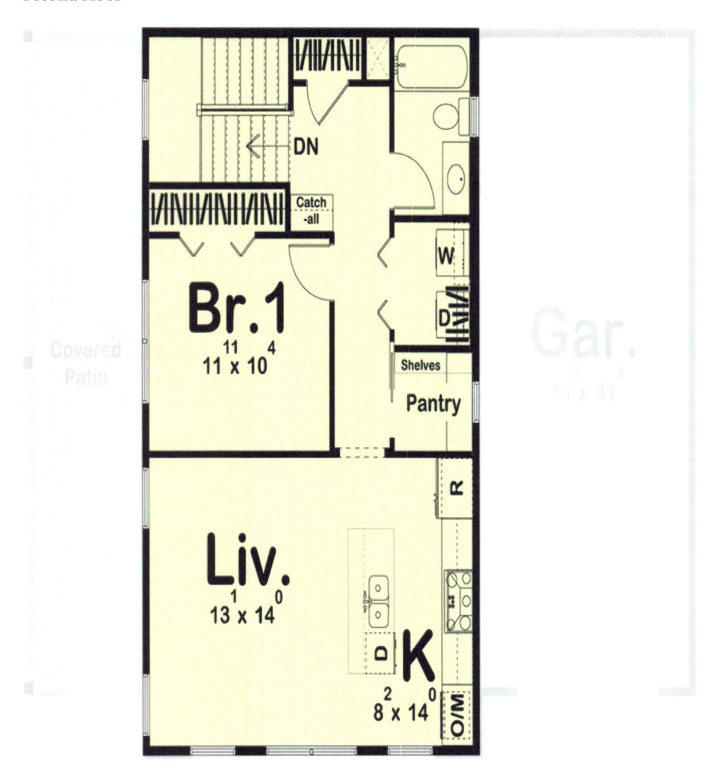

Plan Details

Square Footage Breakdown

Total Heated Area:	767 sq. ft.
2nd Floor:	767 sq. ft.
Covered Patio:	256 sq. ft.

Beds/Baths

Bedrooms:	1
Full Bathrooms:	1

Foundation Type

Standard Foundations:	Slab

Exterior Walls

Standard Type(s):	2x4
Optional Type(s):	2x6

Dimensions

Width:	44' 0"
Depth:	35' 0"
Max Ridge Height:	28' 0"

Garage

Type:	Attached
Area:	1144 sq. ft.
Count:	3 cars
Entry Location:	Front

Ceiling Heights

Floor / Height:	First Floor / 9' 0" Second Floor / 9' 0"

Roof Details

Primary Pitch:	8 On 12
Secondary Pitch:	3 On 12

Three-Bedroom One-Story Modern Farmhouse

REAR ELEVATION - WALKOUT FOUNDATION

| 1,797 | 3 | 2 | 1 | 2 |
| Heated S.F. | Beds | Baths | Stories | Cars |

- The front porch and board-and-batten siding contribute to the aesthetic attractiveness of this one-story modern farmhouse design. In the open kitchen/great room, guests are greeted by a cathedral ceiling and a fireplace.

- The L-shaped kitchen and island are close to the dining area, which extends to a covered patio in the backyard. • The vaulted-ceilinged master suite is tucked away for privacy. • Two bedrooms on the opposite side of the house share a bathroom with a big whirlpool tub, shower, water closet, and walk-in closet with direct access to the laundry area. The third bedroom features an ext**erior view of the covered porch.**

Floor Plan

Main Level

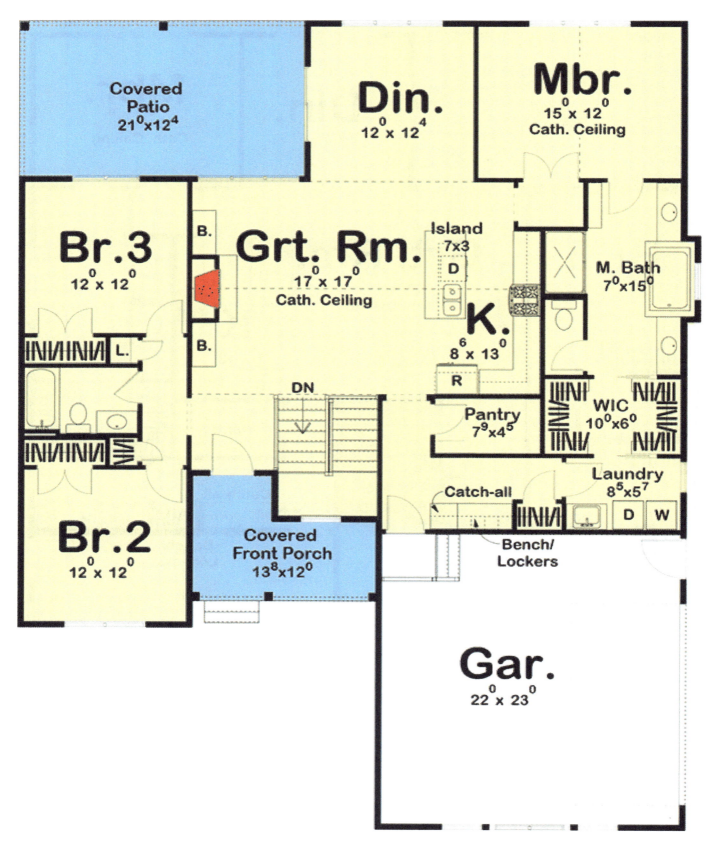

Slab/Crawl Option

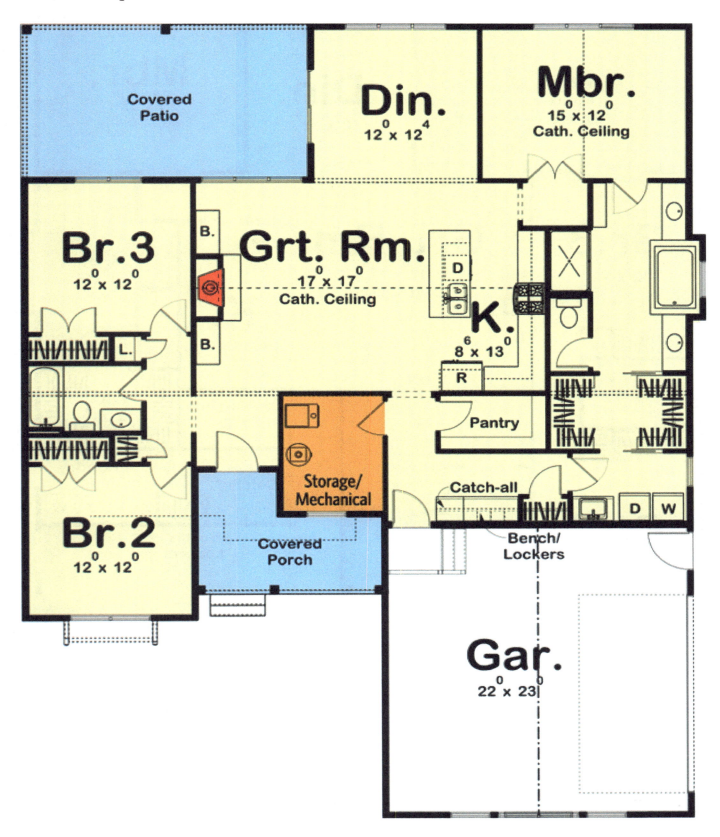

Plan details

Square Footage Breakdown

Total Heated Area:	1,797 sq. ft.
1st Floor:	1,797 sq. ft.
Porch, Rear:	259 sq. ft.
Porch, Front:	106 sq. ft.

Dimensions

Width:	49' 0"
Depth:	64' 0"
Max Ridge Height:	25' 6"

Beds/Baths

Bedrooms:	3
Full Bathrooms:	2

Garage

Type:	Attached
Area:	529 sq. ft.
Count:	2 cars
Entry Location:	Side

Foundation Type

Standard Foundations:	Basement
Optional Foundations:	Slab, Crawl, Walkout

Exterior Walls

Standard Type(s):	2x4
Optional Type(s):	2x6

Roof Details

Primary Pitch:	12 on 12
Secondary Pitch:	8 on 12
Framing Type:	Stick

Barn-Style Garage with Apartment Above

774	1	1	2	3
Heated S.F.	Beds	Baths	Stories	Cars

• The exterior of this garage apartment incorporates board-and-batten siding, sliding wood shutters, 9' by 7' wood garage doors, and a sliding barn door.

• A big two-car garage and a workshop with an overhead door are located on the ground level. A sliding barn door provides access to the covered patio from the workshop. The workshop contains a workbench as well.

• The second-floor living space has an efficient open layout with a U-shaped kitchen and breakfast bar. The dining area is adjacent to the kitchen and boasts a magnificent built-in table with chairs. The master suite has access to the bathroom and a built-in window seat.

Floor Plan

Main Level

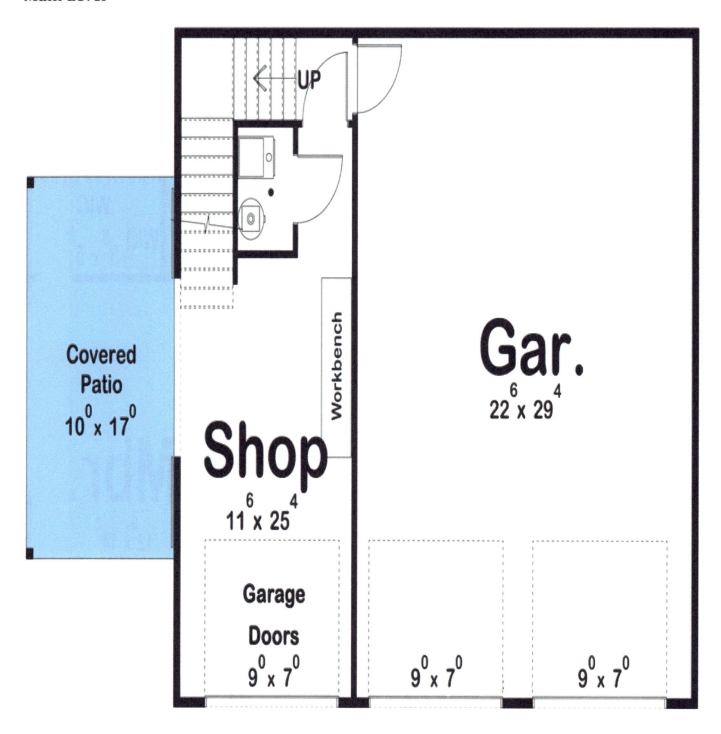

2nd Floor

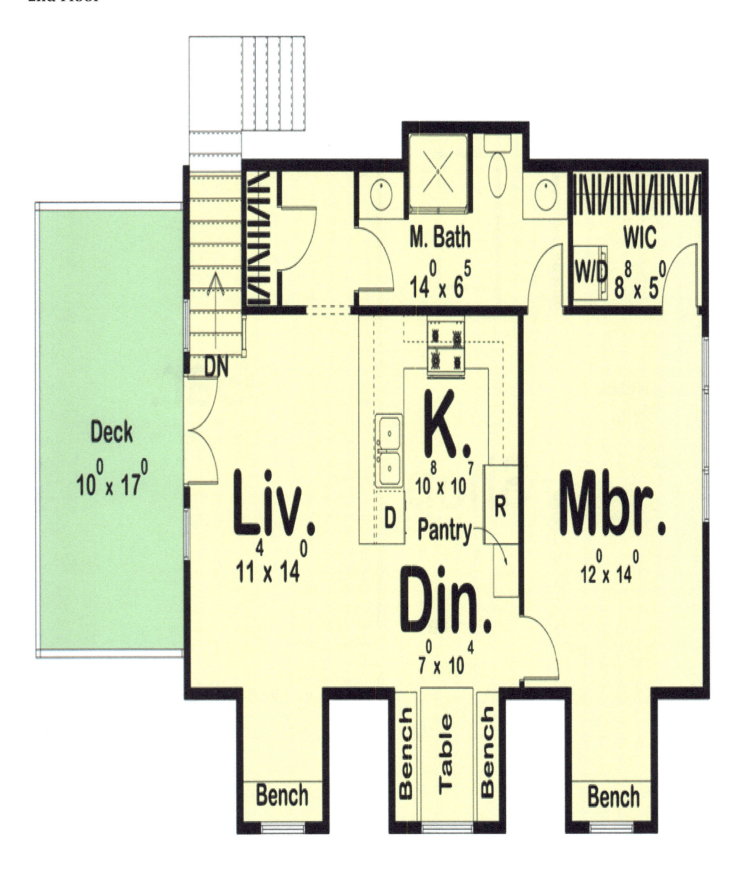

Plan details

Square Footage Breakdown

Total Heated Area:	774 sq. ft.
2nd Floor:	774 sq. ft.
Covered Patio:	170 sq. ft.
Deck:	170 sq. ft.

Dimensions

Width:	45' 0"
Depth:	30' 0"
Max Ridge Height:	26' 0"

Beds/Baths

Bedrooms:	1
Full Bathrooms:	1

Garage

Type:	Detached
Area:	1050 sq. ft.
Count:	3 cars
Entry Location:	Front

Foundation Type

Standard Foundations: Slab

Ceiling Heights

Floor / Height:

First Floor / 9' 0"
Second Floor / 9' 0"

Exterior Walls

Standard Type(s):   2x4

Optional Type(s):   2x6

Roof Details

Primary Pitch: 6 on 12

Secondary Pitch: 22 on 12

Modern Mountain House Plan with Great Room Open to Upstairs Loft

Combining wood siding, stone, and a metal roof for jaw-dropping curb appeal, the modern mountain house design boasts an exquisite front. A garage with a drive-through and a huge bonus room located over the garage accentuate the outside.

A big island with a snack bar and a walk-in pantry complement the kitchen's design. The loft is accessible from the great room, which shares a double-sided fireplace with the kitchen and great room. The master suite is positioned on the main floor for convenience. Large windows in the reading nook of the master suite let in a plenty of natural light. There are two separate vanities, a walk-in shower, and a soaking tub in the master bathroom. Conveniently, the master closet is linked to the laundry room.

The loft space on the second floor of the residence overlooks the living room and is warmed by its fireplace. Additionally, the second story contains three bedrooms. The second and third bedrooms share a bathroom while the fourth bedroom and loft share a bathroom.

The extra 970-square-foot room over the garage is excellent for any activity and expands the concept. The optionally finished 1,519-square-foot basement contains a family room, bar, game room, extra bedroom, and gym room.

Floor Plan

Main Level

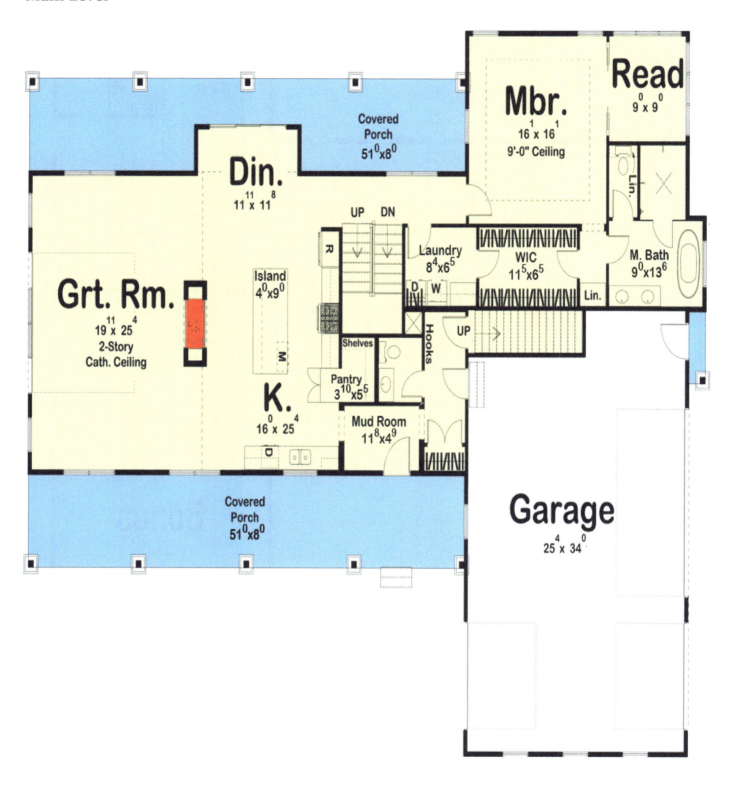

Second Floor

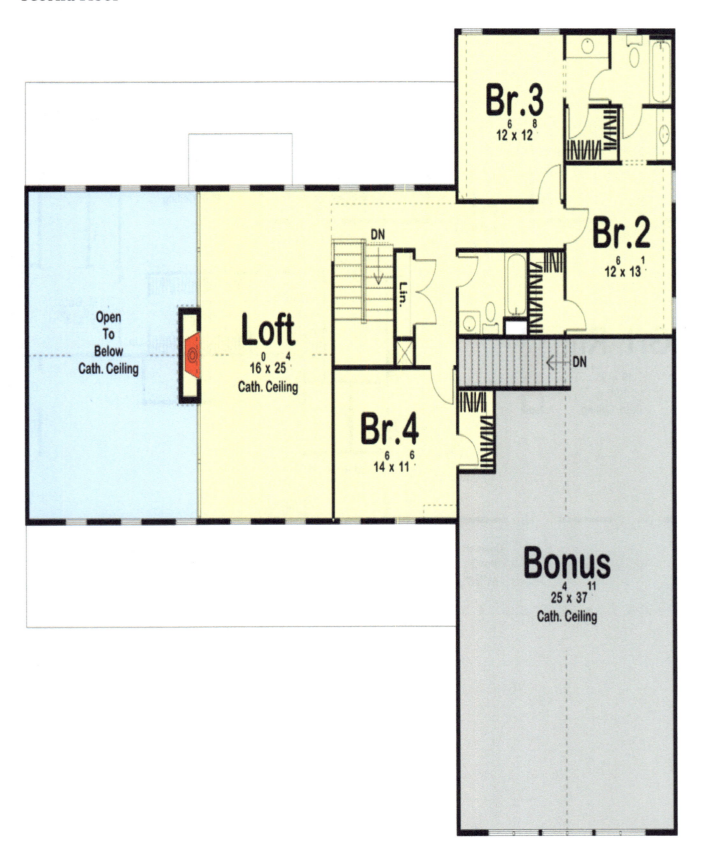

Optional Lower Level(+$250)

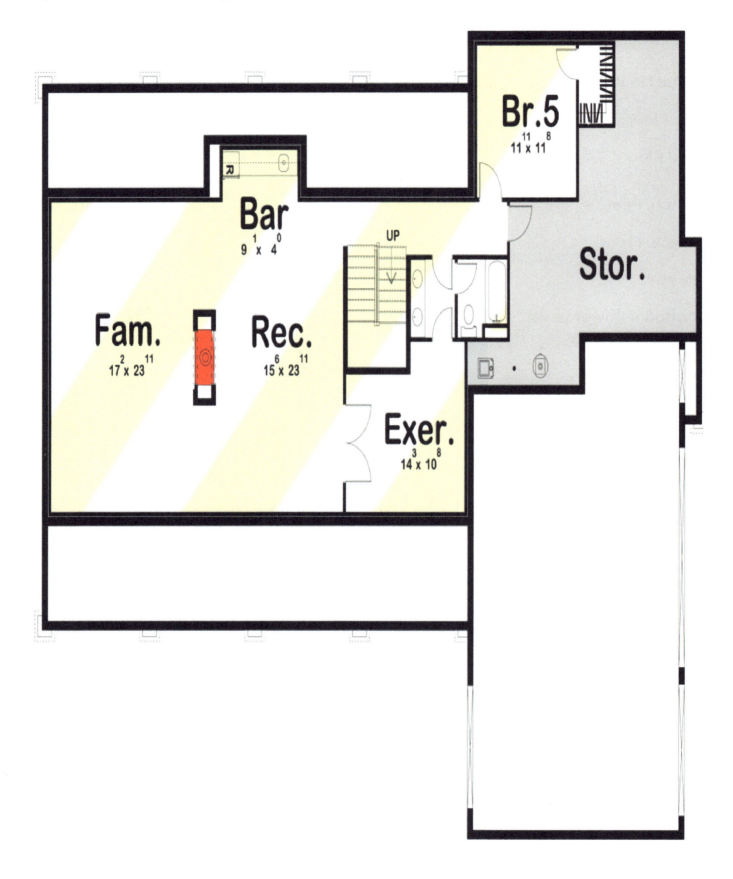

Plan Details

Square Footage Breakdown

Total Heated Area:	3,371 sq. ft.
1st Floor:	2,010 sq. ft.
2nd Floor:	1,361 sq. ft.
Porch, Rear:	359 sq. ft.
Porch, Front:	408 sq. ft.
Bonus:	970 sq. ft.
Optional Lower Level:	1,519 sq. ft.

Beds/Baths

Bedrooms:	4 or 5
Full Bathrooms:	3 or 4
Half Bathrooms:	1

Foundation Type

Standard Foundations:	Basement
Optional Foundations:	Walkout, Slab, Crawl

Exterior Walls

Standard Type(s):	2x4
Optional Type(s):	2x6

Dimensions

Width:	79' 0"
Depth:	62' 0"
Max Ridge Height:	33' 8"

Garage

Type:	Attached
Area:	932 sq. ft.
Count:	3 cars
Entry Location:	Courtyard, Side

Ceiling Heights

Floor / Height:

Lower Level / 9' 0"
First Floor / 9' 0"
Second Floor / 8' 0"

Roof Details

Primary Pitch: 12 On 12

Secondary Pitch: 4 On 12

Rustic Barndominium with Loft Overlooking Great Room Below

• This Rustic Barndominium floor plan offers an open living area that leads into a kitchen facing the rear, making it a great spot for hosting family gatherings.

• A level eating bar at the kitchen island provides a relaxed area to eat or converse, and the back porch is easily accessible for grilling and dining outdoors. • A loft overlooking the living room and a fourth bedroom with access to a full bathroom are placed on the second story.

• The master bedroom is situated on the left side of the layout and has a 5-fixture bathroom and a walk-in closet. The second and third bedrooms share a hall bathroom.

- 2,992 Heated S.F.
- 4 Beds
- 3.5 Baths
- 2 Stories

FLOOR PLAN

Main Level

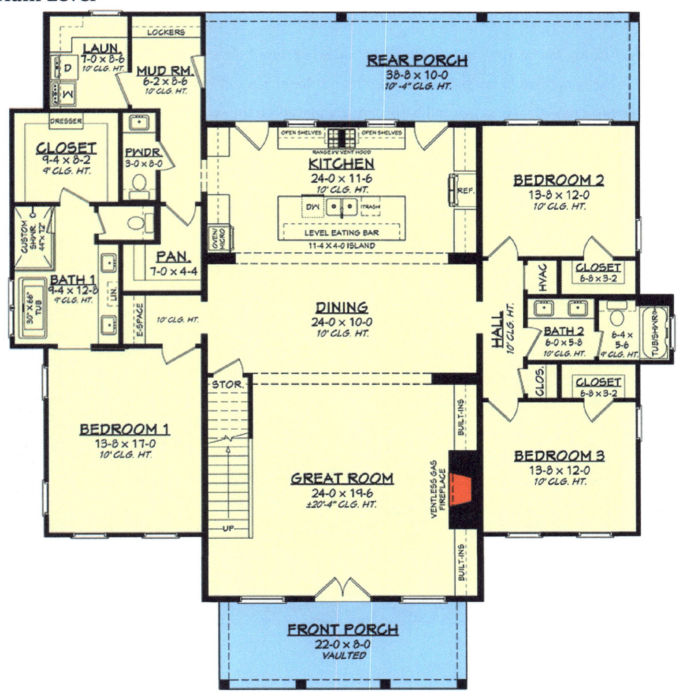

2nd Floor

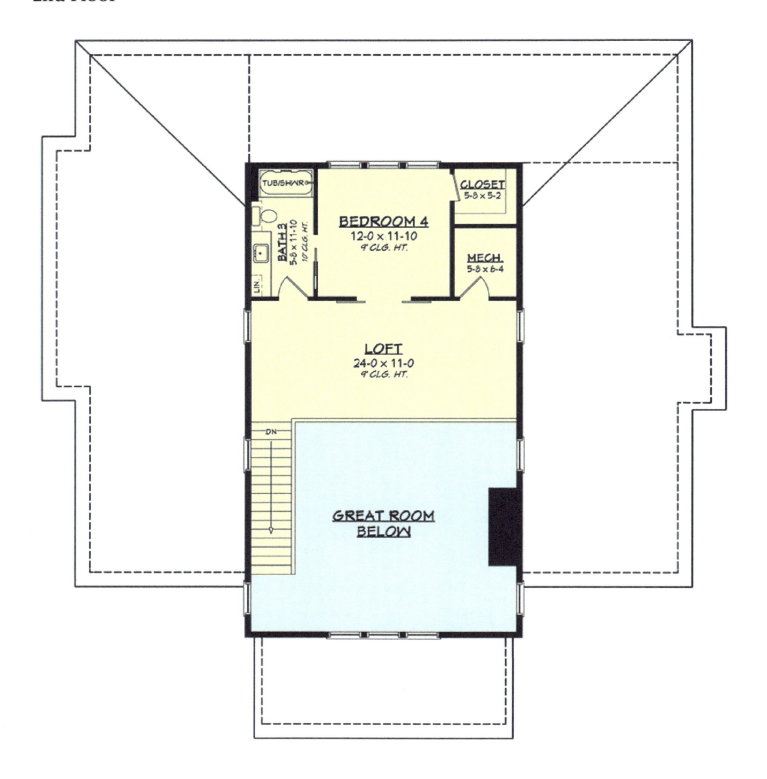

Square Footage Breakdown

Total Heated Area:	2,992 sq. ft.
1st Floor:	2,392 sq. ft.
2nd Floor:	600 sq. ft.
Porch, Rear:	387 sq. ft.
Porch, Front:	176 sq. ft.

Dimensions

Width:	59' 0"
Depth:	62' 0"
Max Ridge Height:	32' 0"

Beds/Baths

Bedrooms:	4
Full Bathrooms:	3
Half Bathrooms:	1

Foundation Type

Standard Foundations:	Crawl, Slab
Optional Foundations:	Basement, Walkout

Exterior Walls

Standard Type(s):	2x4
Optional Type(s):	2x6

Ceiling Heights

Floor / Height:	First Floor / 10' 0" Second Floor / 9' 0"

Roof Details

Primary Pitch:	10 on 12
Secondary Pitch:	4 on 12

Charming Farmhouse Barndominium with Two Bedrooms

1,871	2	2	2	3
Heated S.F.	Beds	Baths	Stories	Cars

• The external craftsmanship of this unique barn-style cottage exudes curb appeal. • The vaulted ceiling in the main living room gives adequate volume, making the space feel open and airy.

• The first bedroom is tucked away just inside the garage, with a full bathroom just across the hall. • The second bedroom, a full bathroom, the laundry room, and a loft overlooking the living space are located on the second level.

A built-in bench and lockers help organize outdoor gear in the mudroom, which is placed just inside the entry to the 3-car garage.

Floor Plan

Main Level

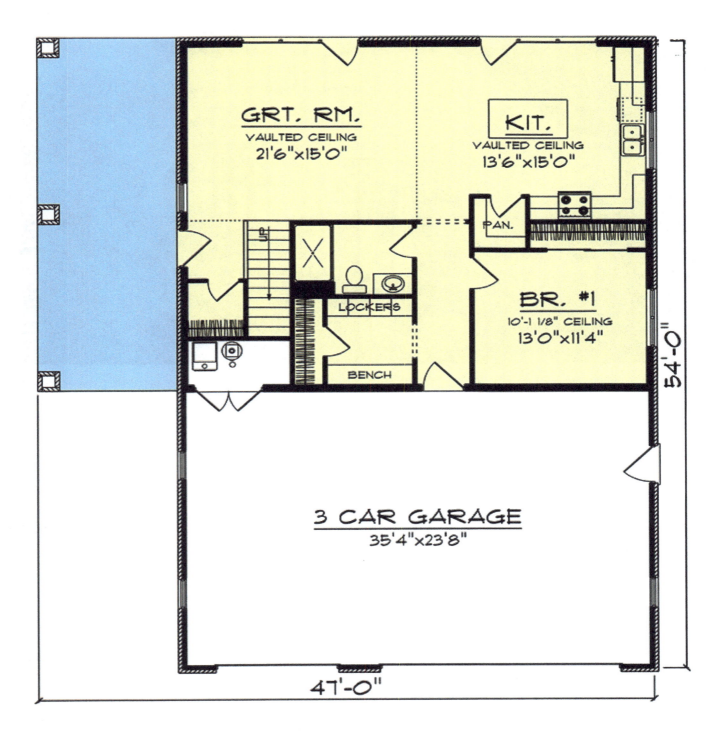

2nd Floor

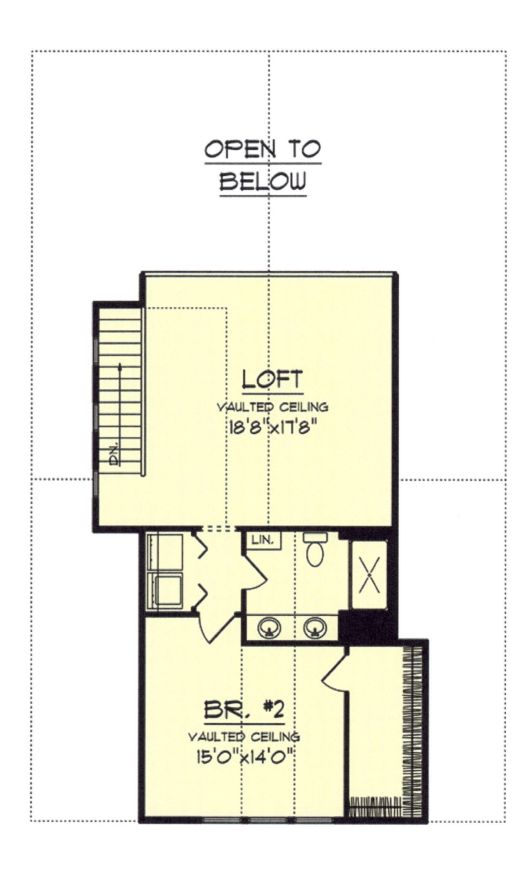

Plan details

Square Footage Breakdown

Total Heated Area:	1,871 sq. ft.
1st Floor:	1,080 sq. ft.
2nd Floor:	791 sq. ft.
Porch, Combined:	337 sq. ft.

Dimensions

Width:	47' 0"
Depth:	54' 0"
Max Ridge Height:	27' 4"

Beds/Baths

Bedrooms:	2
Full Bathrooms:	2

Garage

Type:	Attached
Area:	864 sq. ft.
Count:	3 cars
Entry Location:	Front

Foundation Type

Standard Foundations:	Slab
Optional Foundations:	Crawl

Ceiling Heights

Floor / Height:	First Floor / 10' 0"

Exterior Walls

Standard Type(s):	2x6

Roof Details

Primary Pitch:	10 on 12
Secondary Pitch:	4 on 12
Framing Type:	Truss

Rustic Ranch Home Plan with Cathedral Ceilings and a Broad Front Porch

This magnificent one-story, three-bedroom barndominium home plan offers a rustic façade with stone, wood beams, a metal roof, and board and batten siding.

A spacious covered front porch with a cathedral ceiling beckons you inside, where you will discover a spacious floor layout.

The dining area, kitchen, and family room are arranged beneath a soaring cathedral ceiling, making the space feel large. The fireplace in the family room is bordered by built-in bookcases, and the kitchen island is equipped with a snack bar.

On the left side of the house, the master bedroom is tucked away for solitude and includes a gorgeous tray ceiling. Separate vanities, a linen closet, a private toilet area, and a big walk-in closet are featured in the master bathroom.

Two bedrooms share a centrally-located hall bathroom with two vanities.

1,695 Heated S.F. | 3 Beds | 2 Baths | 1 Stories

FLOOR PLAN

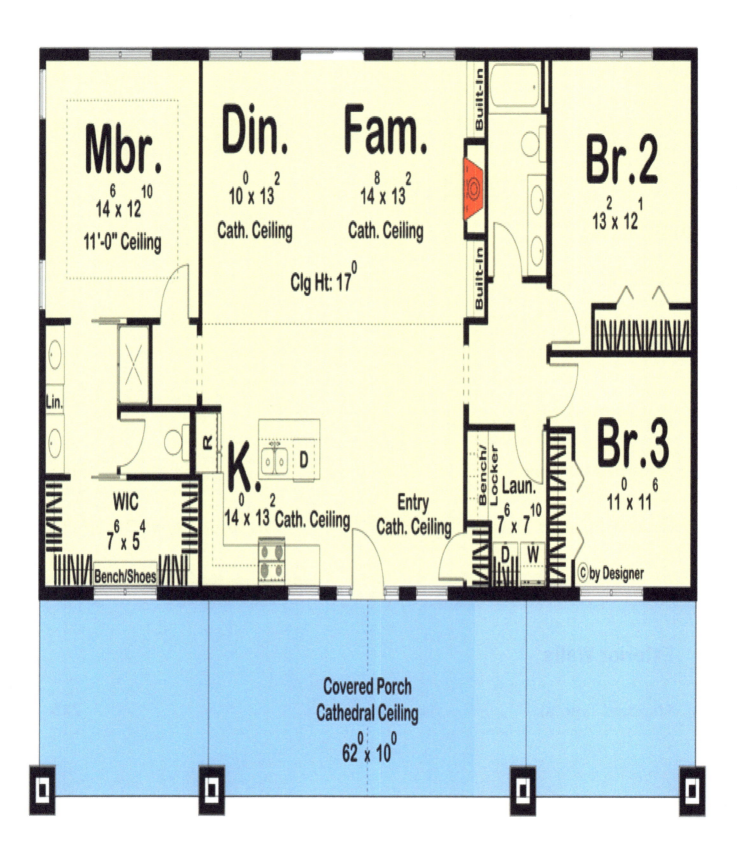

Square Footage Breakdown

Total Heated Area:	1,695 sq. ft.
1st Floor:	1,695 sq. ft.
Porch, Front:	618 sq. ft.

Beds/Baths

Bedrooms:	3
Full Bathrooms:	2

Foundation Type

Standard Foundations:	Slab
Optional Foundations:	Walkout, Crawl, Basement

Exterior Walls

Standard Type(s):	2x6

Dimensions

Width:	62' 0"
Depth:	38' 0"
Max Ridge Height:	21' 0"

Ceiling Heights

Floor / Height:	First Floor / 10' 0"

Roof Details

Primary Pitch:	8 on 12
Secondary Pitch:	3 on 12
Framing Type:	Stick

Rustic Shop House with Vaulted Great Room and Covered Outdoor Spaces

This rustic shousey (a combination of a shop and a house) is ideally suited for usage as an auxiliary living unit, guest or in-law suite, Airbnb or rental property.

On the garage side, there are a 2-car 18' by 9' garage door and a single-car 8' by 9' garage door. Inside is a huge, open space with laundry and mechanicals along the wall dividing the garage from the house and a door in the back corner.

The soaring great room is open to the 13' by 3'6" kitchen island and is fitted with a wood burner. A distinct entrance leads to a covered porch. Dual 8' by 8' quad patio doors provide access to a vaulted covered patio.

A common bathroom completes the bedrooms. This is made with normal 2x6 framing as opposed to steel.

FLOOR PLAN

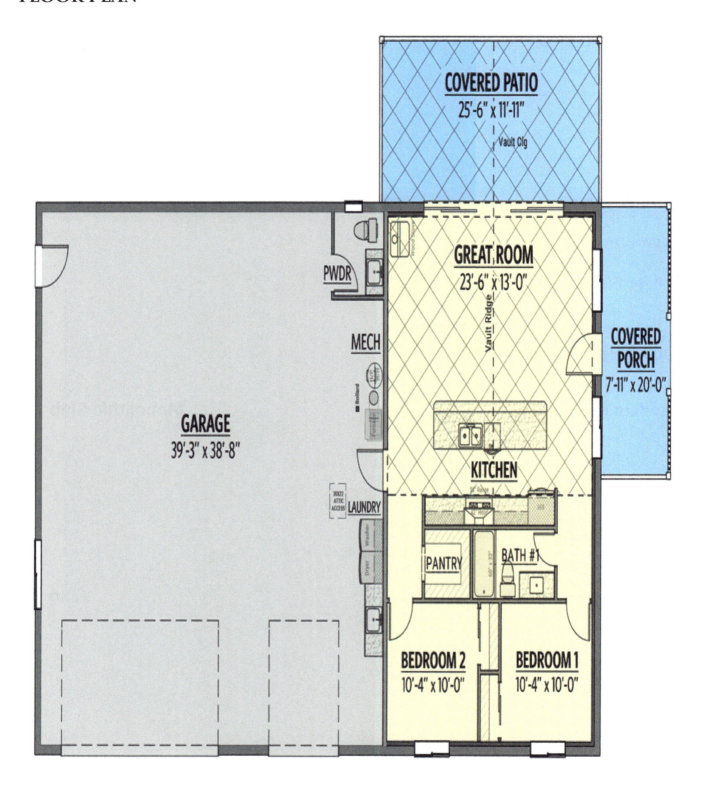

Square Footage Breakdown

Total Heated Area:	1,000 sq. ft.
1st Floor:	1,000 sq. ft.
Covered Patio:	466 sq. ft.

Beds/Baths

Bedrooms:	2
Full Bathrooms:	1

Foundation Type

Standard Foundations:	Monolithic Slab

Exterior Walls

Standard Type(s):	2x6

Dimensions

Width:	72' 0"
Depth:	52' 0"

Garage

Type:	Attached
Area:	1600 sq. ft.
Count:	3 cars
Entry Location:	Side

Ceiling Heights

Floor / Height:	First Floor / 10' 0"

Roof Details

Primary Pitch:	8 on 12
Secondary Pitch:	4 on 12
Framing Type:	Stick And Truss

Barn-Style Garage with Apartment Above

The exterior of this garage apartment design includes board-and-batten siding, sliding wood shutters, 9' by 7' wood garage doors, and a sliding barn door.

A big two-car garage and a workshop with an overhead door are located on the ground level. The covered patio can be accessed from the workshop, which also contains a functional workbench, via a sliding barn door.

The second-floor living room is designed with an efficient open plan, U-shaped kitchen, and breakfast bar. The dining space is adjacent to the kitchen and boasts a magnificent built-in table with seating. The master suite has access to the bathroom and a built-in window seat.

774	1	1	2	3
Heated S.F.	Beds	Baths	Stories	Cars

FLOOR PLAN

Main Level

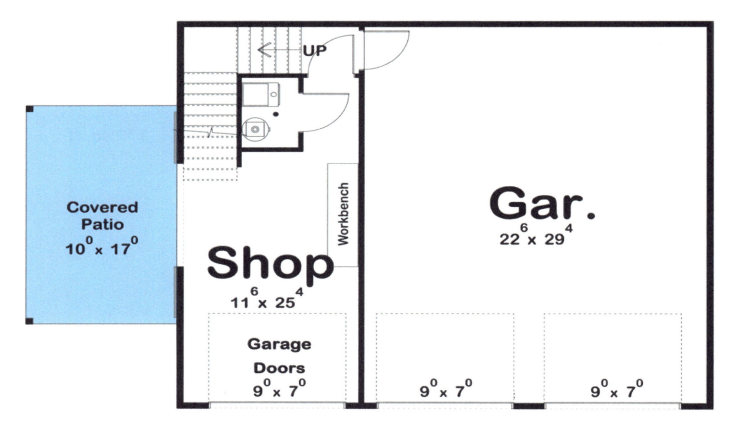

2nd Floor

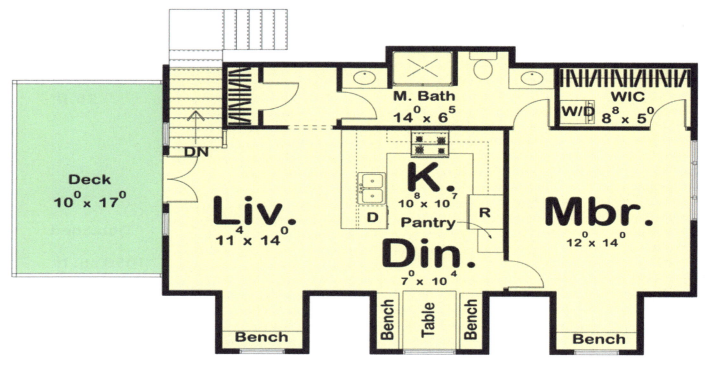

Square Footage Breakdown

Total Heated Area:	774 sq. ft.
2nd Floor:	774 sq. ft.
Covered Patio:	170 sq. ft.
Deck:	170 sq. ft.

Beds/Baths

Bedrooms:	1
Full Bathrooms:	1

Dimensions

Width:	45' 0"
Depth:	30' 0"
Max Ridge Height:	26' 0"

Garage

Type:	Detached
Area:	1050 sq. ft.
Count:	3 cars
Entry Location:	Front

Foundation Type

Standard Foundations: Slab

Exterior Walls

Standard Type(s): 2x4

Optional Type(s): 2x6

Ceiling Heights

Floor / Height:
First Floor / 9' 0"
Second Floor / 9' 0"

Roof Details

Primary Pitch: 6 on 12

Secondary Pitch: 22 on 12

Barndominium with a Front Wrapping Porch

This Barndominium's right elevation features a 36'-deep double garage with an additional overhead door on the rear elevation.

The front porch wraps around to the living room, which extends to the kitchen and is highlighted by a big island with a window facing forward above the kitchen sink.

The master bedroom is located on the main level and is equipped with a full bathroom and direct access to the laundry area.

The entry to the garage connects to a mudroom where gear can be stored.

On the second floor, three bedrooms share a four-fixture bathroom, while a huge loft can serve as a playroom or media room.

- **2,160: Heated S.F. • 4 Beds • 2.5 Baths • 2 Stories • 3 Cars**

FLOOR PLAN

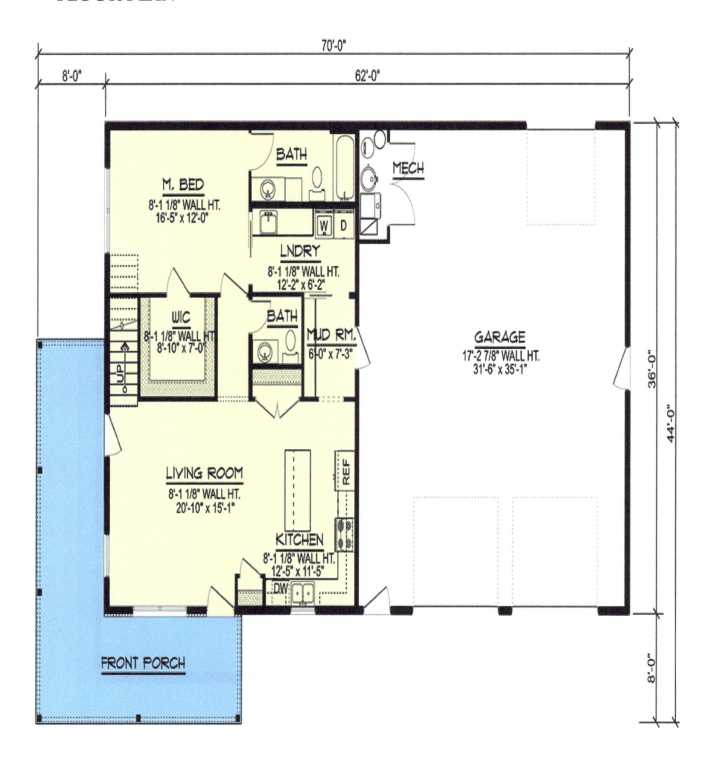

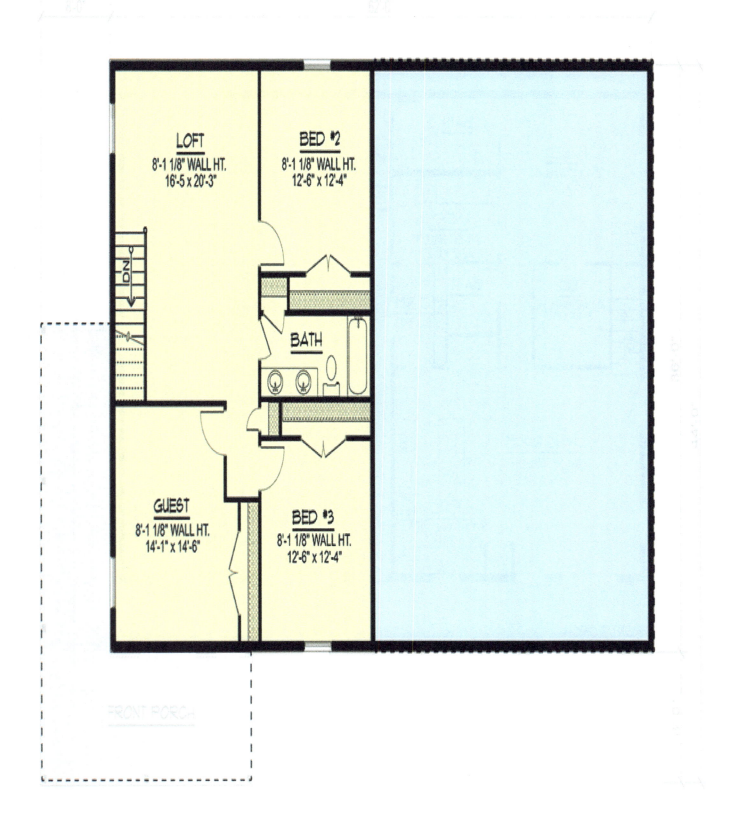

Square Footage Breakdown

Total Heated Area:	2,160 sq. ft.
1st Floor:	1,080 sq. ft.
2nd Floor:	1,080 sq. ft.
Porch, Front:	371 sq. ft.

Beds/Baths

Bedrooms:	4
Full Bathrooms:	2
Half Bathrooms:	1

Foundation Type

Standard Foundations:	Basement, Crawl
Optional Foundations:	Slab, Walkout

Exterior Walls

Standard Type(s):	2x6

Dimensions

Width:	70' 0"
Depth:	44' 0"
Max Ridge Height:	23' 9"

Garage

Type:	Attached
Area:	1152 sq. ft.
Count:	3 cars
Entry Location:	Front

Roof Details

Primary Pitch:	4 on 12
Framing Type:	Truss

Charming Farmhouse Barndominium with Two Bedrooms

1,871 Heated S.F.	**2** Beds	**2** Baths	**2** Stories	**3** Cars

- The exterior craftsmanship of this distinctive, barn-style cabin exudes curb appeal.
- The vaulted ceiling in the main living area provides ample volume, making the space feel spacious and airy.
- The first bedroom is tucked away just inside the garage, with convenient access to the full bathroom just across the hall.
- The second bedroom, a complete bathroom, the laundry room, and a spacious loft overlooking the living area are located on the second floor.
- A built-in bench and lockers assist in organizing outdoor gear in the mudroom, which is located just inside the 3-car garage's entrance.

Floor Plan

Main Level

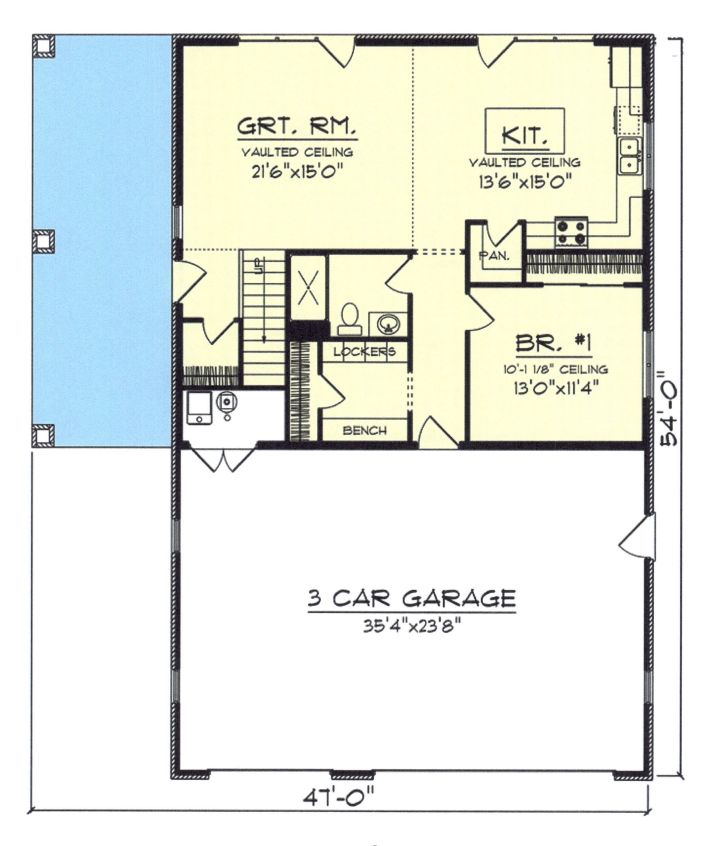

2nd Floor

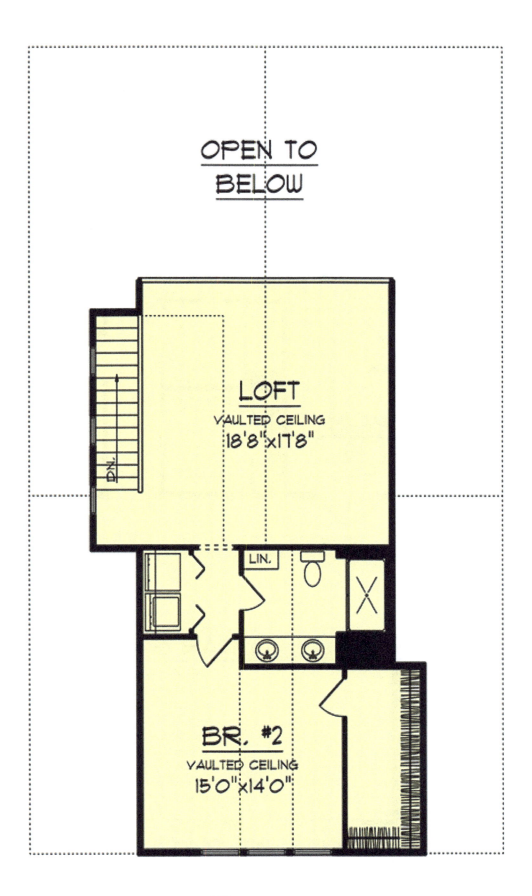

Plan details

Square Footage Breakdown

Total Heated Area:	1,871 sq. ft.
1st Floor:	1,080 sq. ft.
2nd Floor:	791 sq. ft.
Porch, Combined:	337 sq. ft.

Dimensions

Width:	47' 0"
Depth:	54' 0"
Max Ridge Height:	27' 4"

Beds/Baths

Bedrooms:	2
Full Bathrooms:	2

Garage

Type:	Attached
Area:	864 sq. ft.
Count:	3 cars
Entry Location:	Front

Foundation Type

Standard Foundations:	Slab
Optional Foundations:	Crawl

Ceiling Heights

Floor / Height:	First Floor / 10' 0"

Exterior Walls

Standard Type(s):	2x6

Roof Details

Primary Pitch:	10 on 12
Secondary Pitch:	4 on 12
Framing Type:	Truss

Expanded Barn-Style Garage with Tractor Port

The 48' x 48' proportions of this barn-style garage provide space for eight automobiles, while the board-and-batten siding and corrugated metal roof give the building a contemporary look.

In the structure's rear, beneath a shed roof, is a tractor port that provides covered storage for your heavy equipment.

The loft's vaulted ceiling gives enough storage space upstairs.

- 0 Heated S.F.   • 0 Beds   • 2 Stories   • 2 Cars

FLOOR PLAN

Main Level

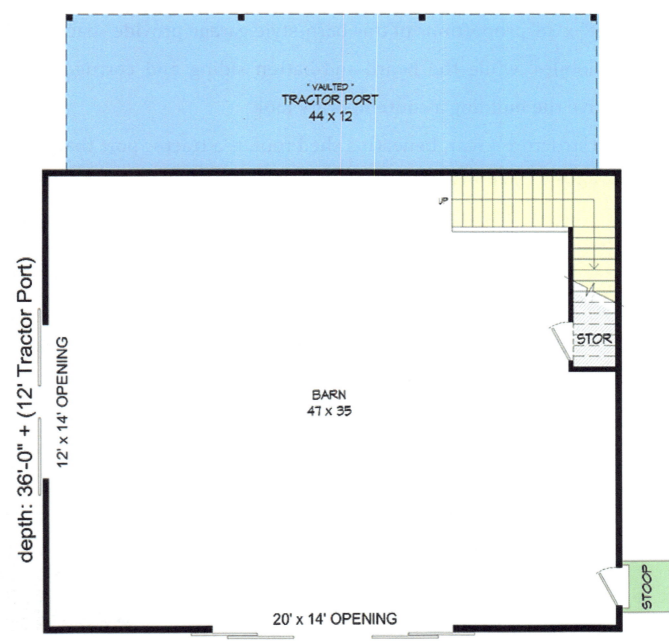

2nd Floor

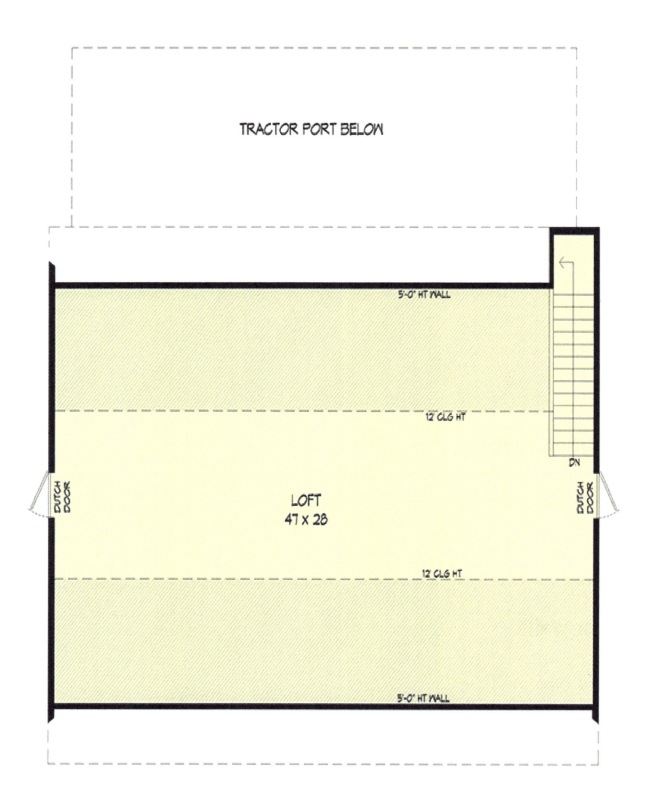

Plan details

Square Footage Breakdown

Total Heated Area:	0 sq. ft.
2nd Floor:	1,372 sq. ft.

Beds/Baths

Bedrooms:	0

Foundation Type

Standard Foundations:	Slab

Exterior Walls

Standard Type(s):	2x6

Dimensions

Width:	48' 0"
Depth:	48' 0"
Max Ridge Height:	34' 10"

Garage

Type:	Detached
Area:	1728 sq. ft.
Count:	2 cars
Entry Location:	Front

Ceiling Heights

Floor / Height:	First Floor / 15' 0" Second Floor / 12' 0"

Roof Details

Primary Pitch:	10 on 12
Secondary Pitch:	5 on 12
Framing Type:	Stick

The Garage Resembles A Barn With A Vaulted Workshop, Dog Run, Side Porch, And Bonus Space

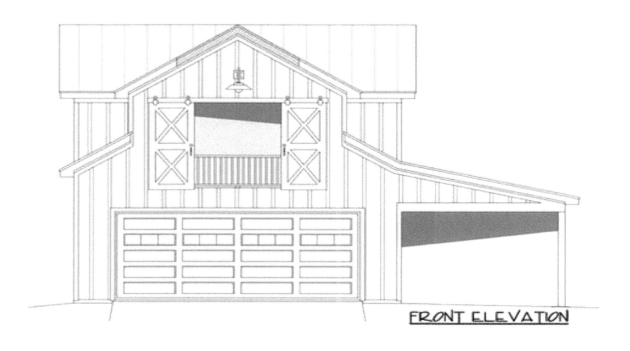
FRONT ELEVATION

LEFT ELEVATION

REAR ELEVATION

RIGHT ELEVATION

1,031
Heated S.F.

0
Beds

1
Baths

2
Stories

2
Cars

Floor Plan

Main Level

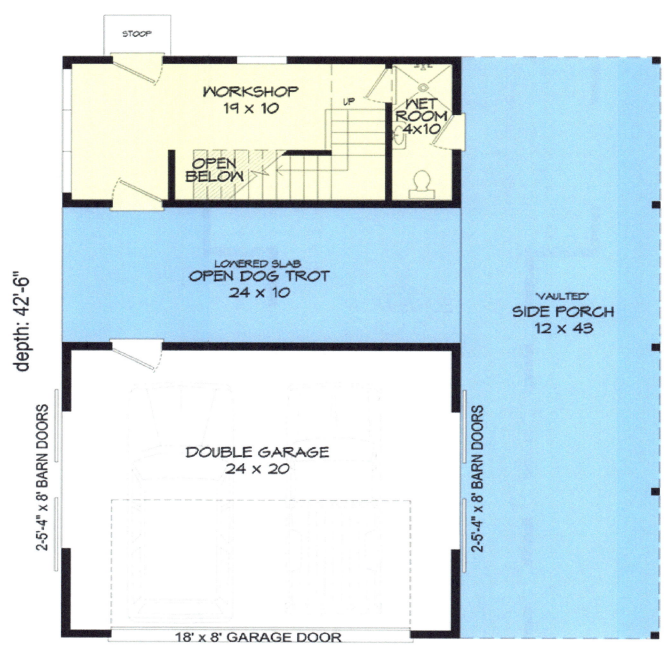

2nd Floor

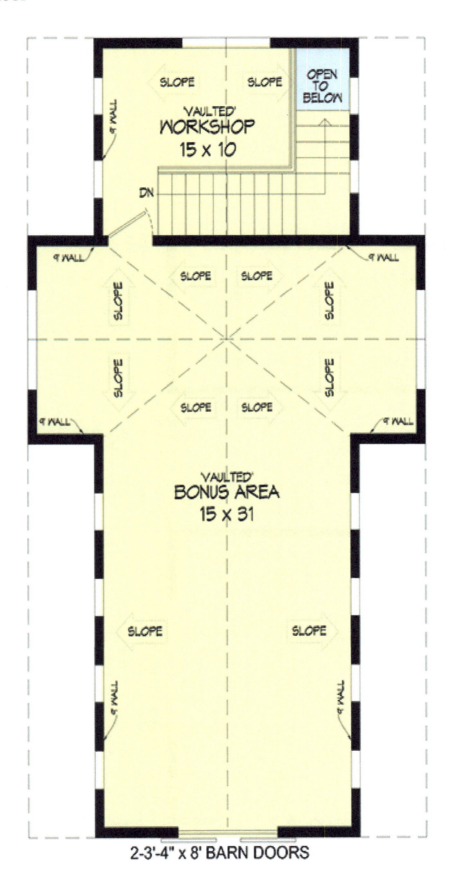

Plan details

Square Footage Breakdown

Total Heated Area:	1,031 sq. ft.
1st Floor:	264 sq. ft.
2nd Floor:	767 sq. ft.
Porch, Combined:	510 sq. ft.

Dimensions

Width:	36' 0"
Depth:	42' 6"
Max Ridge Height:	25' 1"

Beds/Baths

Bedrooms:	0
Full Bathrooms:	1

Garage

Area:	516 sq. ft.
Count:	2 cars
Entry Location:	Front

Foundation Type

Standard Foundations:	Slab

Ceiling Heights

Floor / Height:

First Floor / 9' 0"
Second Floor / 9' 0"

Exterior Walls

Standard Type(s): 2x4

Optional Type(s): 2x6

Roof Details

Primary Pitch: 8 on 12

Framing Type: Stick

Exclusive 5-Bedroom Modern Farmhouse Plan with Upstairs Master Suite and Laundry

The wraparound porch, dramatic metal roof, and two-car garage of this contemporary farmhouse provide a breath of fresh country air.

The private den, located immediately off the entryway, functions as a guest retreat. A huge great room with a fireplace and plenty natural light is connected to the kitchen and dining room. Beyond the kitchen's sliding door are more alternatives for outdoor entertaining.

The interior French doors on the upper level lead to a master suite with a vaulted ceiling, a 5-piece master bath, and a big walk-in closet. Enjoy the convenience of a laundry facility on the second floor.

Two additional bedrooms and a full bathroom are located across the hall and are excellent for family or friends.

The stylish bonus room with vaulted ceilings has endless potential.

- 2,376 Heated S.F.   • 5 Beds   • 3 Baths   • 2 Stories   • 2 Cars

Floor Plan

Main Level

2nd Floor

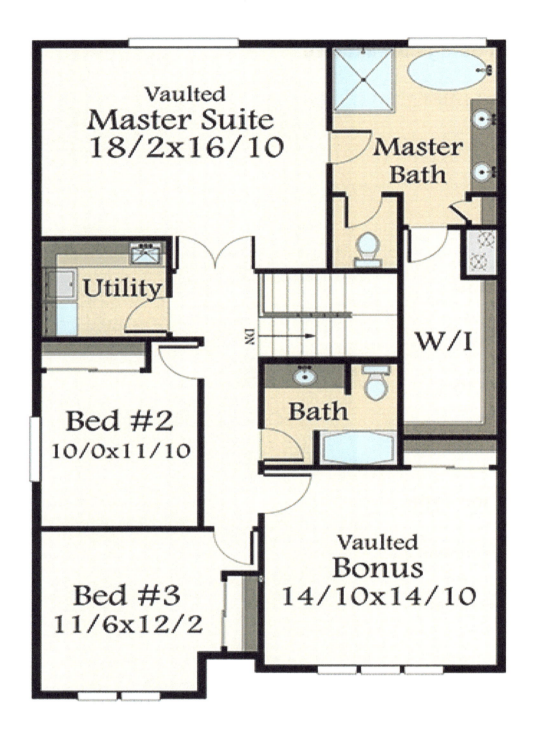

Plan details

Square Footage Breakdown

Total Heated Area:	2,376 sq. ft.
1st Floor:	974 sq. ft.
2nd Floor:	1,402 sq. ft.

Beds/Baths

Bedrooms:	5
Full Bathrooms:	3

Foundation Type

Standard Foundations:	Crawl
Optional Foundations:	Basement

Exterior Walls

Standard Type(s):	2x6

Dimensions

Width:	34' 6"
Depth:	45' 0"

Garage

Type:	Attached
Area:	431 sq. ft.
Count:	2 cars
Entry Location:	Front

4-Bed Country Craftsman Plan with Open Concept Living Space

This Country Craftsman home design with a 27' width is ideal for tight lots, as it offers an attractive facade, four bedrooms on the second floor, and a carport between the double garage and the main house.

The large front porch leads to an open-concept living area with a fireplace anchoring the left wall.

A coat closet near each of the rear doors that go to the carport facilitates the organization of your outdoor gear, while an exterior storage room is great for storing lawn equipment and supplies.

The master bedroom is placed in the rear of the second level, adjacent to a bathroom with four fixtures and two walk-in closets. The second floor continues with a laundry room and a loft with access to the last three family bedrooms.

• 2,345 Heated S.F.   • 4 Beds   • 2.5 Baths • 2 Stories • 2-3 Cars

Floor Plan

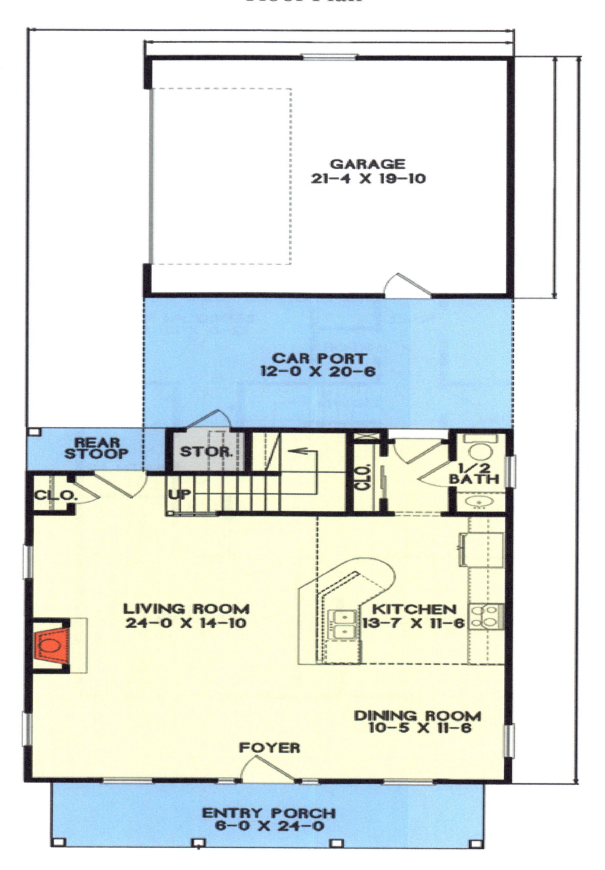

2nd Floor

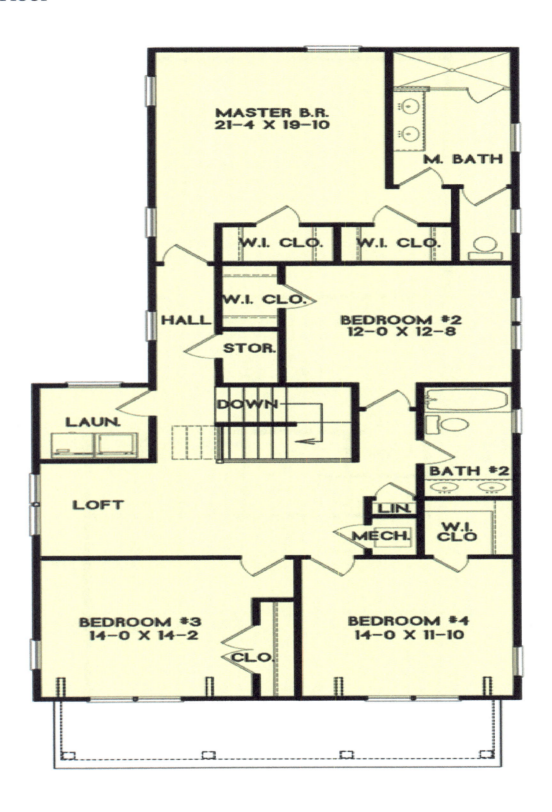

Plan details

Square Footage Breakdown

Total Heated Area:	2,345 sq. ft.
1st Floor:	839 sq. ft.
2nd Floor:	1,506 sq. ft.
Porch, Combined:	175 sq. ft.
Carport:	246 sq. ft.

Beds/Baths

Bedrooms:	4
Full Bathrooms:	2
Half Bathrooms:	1

Foundation Type

Standard Foundations:	Slab

Exterior Walls

Standard Type(s):	2x4

Dimensions

Width:	27' 0"
Depth:	66' 4"
Max Ridge Height:	31' 1"

Garage

Type:	Carport, Attached
Area:	451 sq. ft.
Count:	2 or 3 cars
Entry Location:	Side

Ceiling Heights

Floor / Height:	First Floor / 9' 0" Second Floor / 8' 0"

Roof Details

Primary Pitch:	8 on 12
Secondary Pitch:	8 on 12
Framing Type:	Stick

Made in the USA
Monee, IL
03 July 2023

38448773R00083